TO FLOAT IN THE SPACE BETWEEN

THE
BAGLEY
WRIGHT
LECTURE
SERIES

TERRANCE HAYES

TO FLOAT IN
THE SPACE
BETWEEN

A Life and Work in Conversation with

the Life and Work of Etheridge Knight

WAVE BOOKS

SEATTLE AND NEW YORK

Published by Wave Books

www.wavepoetry.com

Wave Books titles are distributed to the trade by

Consortium Book Sales and Distribution

Phone: 800-283-3572 / SAN 631-760X

Library of Congress Cataloging-in-Publication Data

Names: Hayes, Terrance, author.

Title: To float in the space between : a life and work in conversation with

the life and work of Etheridge Knight / Terrance Hayes.

Description: First edition. | Seattle : Wave Books, [2018] | Series: Bagley

Wright Lecture Series | Includes bibliographical references.

Identifiers: LCCN 2017060740 | ISBN 9781940696614 (trade pbk.)

Subjects: LCSH: Knight, Etheridge, 1931–1991—Criticism and interpretation. |

African American poets.

Classification: LCC PS3561.N45 Z55 2018 | DDC 811/.54—dc23

LC record available at https://lccn.loc.gov/2017060740

Designed by Quemadura

Printed in the United States of America

9 8 7 6 5 4 3 2 1

First Edition

FOR FRAN QUINN, FOR THIS BEGINNING

AND CONSTANT UNFOLDING

TO FLOAT IN THE SPACE BETWEEN

THE IDEA OF ANCESTRY

ETHERIDGE KNIGHT

1

Taped to the wall of my cell are 47 pictures: 47 black
faces: my father, mother, grandmothers (1 dead), grandfathers (both dead), brothers, sisters, uncles, aunts,
cousins (1st & 2nd), nieces, and nephews. They stare
across the space at me sprawling on my bunk. I know   5
their dark eyes, they know mine. I know their style,
they know mine. I am all of them, they are all of me;
they are farmers, I am a thief, I am me, they are thee.

I have at one time or another been in love with my mother,
1 grandmother, 2 sisters, 2 aunts (1 went to the asylum),   10
and 5 cousins. I am now in love with a 7-yr-old niece
(she sends me letters written in large block print, and
her picture is the only one that smiles at me).

I have the same name as 1 grandfather, 3 cousins, 3 nephews,
and 1 uncle. The uncle disappeared when he was 15, just took   15
off and caught a freight (they say). He's discussed each year
when the family has a reunion, he causes uneasiness in

the clan, he is an empty space. My father's mother, who is 93
and who keeps the Family Bible with everbody's birth dates
(and death dates) in it, always mentions him. There is no
place in her Bible for "whereabouts unknown."

2

Each fall the graves of my grandfathers call me, the brown
hills and red gullies of mississippi send out their electric
messages, galvanizing my genes. Last yr / like a salmon quitting
the cold ocean-leaping and bucking up his birthstream / I
hitchhiked my way from LA with 16 caps in my pocket and a
monkey on my back. And I almost kicked it with the kinfolks.
I walked barefooted in my grandmother's backyard / I smelled the old
land and the woods / I sipped cornwhiskey from fruit jars with the men /
I flirted with the women / I had a ball till the caps ran out
and my habit came down. That night I looked at my grandmother
and split / my guts were screaming for junk / but I was almost
contented / I had almost caught up with me.
(The next day in Memphis I cracked a croaker's crib for a fix.)

This yr there is a gray stone wall damming my stream, and when
the falling leaves stir my genes, I pace my cell or flop on my bunk
and stare at 47 black faces across the space. I am all of them,
they are all of me, I am me, they are thee, and I have no children
to float in the space between.

LINE 1: TAPED TO
THE WALL OF MY CELL

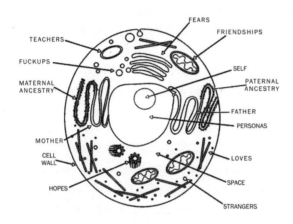

As we study the life and lineage of a particular adult cell, we ask the same questions that a biographer asks of her subject: what were the critical decisions that defined the trajectory of this life, and when were they made? What was the contribution of neighbors, and what role was played by more distant influences? What was the role of chance? At what point was the final fate initially specified, and when was it ultimately sealed? In essence, we would like to understand the molecular biography of the cell.

DAVID A. SHAYWITZ AND DOUGLAS A. MELTON,
"The Molecular Biography of the Cell"

3

WHAT WERE THE CRITICAL DECISIONS THAT DEFINED THE TRAJECTORY OF THIS LIFE?

When I began collecting interviews and stories about Etheridge Knight more than a decade ago, I said, mostly to the few people I cornered for interviews, that I'd never write a biography because it would take more than a decade to do it. This is not a biography. But perhaps it will encourage a future Knight biographer. Consider this a collection of essays as speculative, motley, and adrift as Knight himself. His various personas grace the book covers that are at any given moment resting beside my bed or on my desk. The bespectacled Knight in a prison cell on the back of 1968's *Poems from Prison*; the nappy bohemian Knight on the cover of 1973's *Belly Song and Other Poems*; the Mississippi Knight in cap and overalls on the cover of 1980's *Born of a Woman: New and Selected Poems*; and the sober intellectual Knight on the cover of 1986's *The Essential Etheridge Knight*. Because he has been on my mind for virtually all my writing life, he has appeared from time to time among my poems: influencing perspective (as in "Poet Dying at the Window," from my first book), influencing voice (as in "The Blue Etheridge," from my third book), influencing form (as in "Portrait of Etheridge Knight in the Style of a Crime Report," from my fifth book). Each time I've returned to my work on Knight between publications of my own poetry books, only the impossibility of a biography has remained consistent. He remains both a muse and mystery.

4

ABOUT THE AUTHOR

"I died in Korea from a shrapnel wound and narcotics resurrected me. I died in 1960 from a prison sentence and poetry brought me back to life." Thus Etheridge Knight, who writes from Indiana State Prison, explains how he came to write poetry.

Mr. Knight, whose *Poems from Prison* is his first book of verse, is making a growing reputation with his poems and short stories, which have appeared in *Negro Digest, Journal of Black Poetry, The Lakeshore Outlook, Prison Magazine,* and other periodicals, and in the anthologies *For Malcolm X* and *Potere Negro (Black Power),* published in Italy.

His *Lettere delle Prigione* will be published in Italy this year. Meanwhile, he is writing a novel on the slave revolt in South Carolina led by Denmark Vesey.

Poems from Prison, with its portraits of prisoners such as Hard Rock, who poisoned a guard with syphilitic spit; its sensitive haiku; its love poems; and its poems on Malcolm X, Dinah Washington, Langston Hughes, and Gwendolyn Brooks, shows the range and power of this poet's art.

Poems from Prison, by Etheridge Knight—$1.00

Broadside Press, 12651 Old Mill Place, Detroit, Michigan 48238

ETHERIDGE KNIGHT

POEMS
FROM
PRISON

PREFACE BY GWENDOLYN BROOKS

BROADSIDE PRESS, DETROIT $1.00

$1.75

Belly Song

and other poems

by Etheridge Knight

Etheridge Knight

Born of a Woman

New and Selected Poems

THE ESSENTIAL
ETHERIDGE
KNIGHT

Etheridge Knight

WHEN WERE THE CRITICAL DECISIONS THAT DEFINED THE TRAJECTORY OF THIS LIFE MADE?

At some point in my years wandering/wondering in and between the lines of "The Idea of Ancestry," I began to think of myself as a real-life Charles Kinbote, the deranged scholar in Vladimir Nabokov's *Pale Fire* (1962). Except where Kinbote is literally a mad professor unraveling a 999-line poem by his neighbor-poet, the murdered John Shade, I'm me: a poet, a brother, a southerner unraveling "The Idea of Ancestry," a poem by Etheridge Knight. The distinction between a *scholar* on the trail of a poet and a *poet* on the trail of a poet is an important one. The scholar looks upon his subject as if through a window. The scholar aims to frame the poet's work according to things like genre, talent, culture, history. A clear pane of logic, interpretation, and appreciation separates him from his subject. Conversely, a poet looking upon the poetry of another poet sees something of himself reflected in the pane. Process, imitation, and competition are reflected in the work. A poet looks upon the work of another poet not only through a window but also through a mirror. (Please forgive my generalizations.) What's odd about Charles Kinbote is (1) he believes the window is a mirror—he sees only himself when he looks into it—and (2) he means to lift the window and climb, as a Peeping Tom (or Goldilocks) would, into the lines of his subject. He sees himself everywhere in the poem. Any interpretation of the poem is hogtied to the interpreter. The great, distorting power of Kinbote's imagination gives Nabokov's novel its tension and trajectory. Lampooning the practice of "close reading," *Pale Fire* shows how "expertise" slides down a slippery slope into delusion. Delusion, depending on how you look at it, is a form of the imagination. Can imagination be a form of critical study? For more than a decade I have been imagining my way into the slants and shades of Etheridge Knight.

In 2005, I interviewed Knight's sister Eunice Knight-Bowens during my visit to Indianapolis to read in her 14th Annual Etheridge Knight Festival. The reading took place in a suburban mall in Indianapolis. Eunice had inaugurated the festival in 1992, a year after her brother's death from cancer. The roster included local poets who knew Knight, local high school students who might be the next Etheridge Knight, and poets like me who were drawn by Knight's ghost: Sonia Sanchez, his ex-wife; Amiri Baraka, his peer; groups of brother poets like John Murillo and Reginald Dwayne Betts. After a twenty-year run the festival ended in 2012, a year before Eunice passed away. What was the contribution of neighbors? The festival was made of, by, and for the neighbors of Indianapolis. Etheridge's Indianapolis, Eunice's Indianapolis. When Eunice looked into the window of her brother's poetry she saw her own stories reflected. Did she know from the get-go that her brother was a great, rare kind of poet? I can't say. I know she was happy that I came asking for stories. She put me up in a hotel Knight used to frequent. She said all the black writers met there to talk art and literature, but I was imagining all the booze, tobacco, and jive. The hotel room smelled of the cabbage she brought me and the cigarettes we smoked. I pushed the button on a small tape recorder. "I want people just to tell their stories about Knight, and everything is to come out of those stories," I told Eunice. She didn't miss a beat:

"A lot of his poems, like 'The Idea of Ancestry,' were written while he was in prison, in 'the belly of the beast' as he called it," she said almost automatically. I now know she'd told the story behind the poem many times. So had her brother. "He memorized it, he said, to save his sanity. The aunts were true, the cousins. It's just a true poem."

Some of what she said contradicted what I'd read about Knight's incarceration, some of what she said complicated what I'd read about his life. Knight may well be chief contributor to the lopsided details surrounding his life before imprisonment. Around whatever was his essential, inexplicable self were several identities: southerner, black, son, male, convict, poet. Around those identities were also several biographical holes, gaps, and mysteries. He was the third of seven children and third son of Etheridge Sr. and Belzora Cozart-Knight. I did not ask Eunice why he, and not one of his older brothers, Charles and Floydell, was named after his father. Regrettably, I did not interview any of his other living siblings. His mother and father were dead by then, his brother Charles and sister Lois were dead by then. I sat in one chair and Eunice sat in the other. She wore a blue headscarf and a skin the shade of her brother's skin. She and her brother, she said, came from a long line of storytellers.

"My mother said that when they were little, before they went out to do their chores and before they went to school every morning, her oldest brother, my uncle Cid, played the organ and they had to sing. And so my mother could sing 'do re mi' without music, and so every morning before they went out to do their chores and before they went to school, they had to sing music as an art."

A sharp biographer will definitely need to find all of Knight's surviving relatives, his lovers and ex-lovers, his students, his son, Isaac BuShie Blackburn-Knight. I interviewed Mary Karr, who was one of Knight's students. I've interviewed his editor, Ed Ochester. I've interviewed and gossiped with or made plans to interview and gossip with maybe half a dozen other friends of Knight over the years. I've come nowhere close to gathering enough "facts" for a biography. I have not examined Knight's prison or war records; I have not interviewed inmates or staff at the jails and prisons; I have not interviewed the students of the Free People's Workshop. What was the contribution of neighbors? I have not interviewed his teammates on the army football team in Korea, the soldiers within earshot of his jive and tirades, the nurses who nursed him in rehab, the junkies or pushers who knew him. I have not interviewed Knight's lovers: Sonia Sanchez, Mary McAnally, Evelyn Brown, Elizabeth McKim, Charlene Blackburn. Knight's future biographer will have a lengthy chapter on romance. If we are lucky, someday some future biographer will land in Indianapolis and rent a small car and buy a map on his way to the Indiana State Prison or the factory where Knight worked as a punch-press operator during the five months of his parole or to 555 Massachusetts Avenue where Knight died in 1991 of lung cancer. If the future biographer's book is made into a movie, one hopes tropes of the blues and bluesman don't simplify Knight's life. It's an unreasonable hope, maybe. A life has to be simplified if it is to have shape, arc, trajectory: a biography needs a plot. Knight's story doesn't require much, I suppose. A couple of visits to Corinth, Mississippi, where he was born. To Paducah, Kentucky. I once thought a life was simply the accumulation of ideas, but now I think it may simply be the accumulation of details. Somewhere between detail and idea is the truth. Knight was often blowing smoke, as they say. And to write a biography one would need to gather all that smoke into something solid, something you could hold and turn over in your hands. "The Idea of Ancestry" almost suggests the *idea* of a biography is better than an actual biography.

Influence is never distant. Or influence is always distant. This text is about influence. Biographies mean to spell out influence—an impossible task. I felt I had two choices: a rigorously researched biography or a rigorously imagined biography. I imagine the black poet Etheridge Knight was influenced by the black poet Langston Hughes, for example. But, hell, I can imagine Hughes was a distant influence on every black poet for the last fifty or so years. In the late eighties right about the time I was a sophomore writing a research paper on Hughes, scholar Arnold Rampersad was publishing his encyclopedic, two-volume, nearly 1,000-page biography on Hughes. Despite reams of source material, treks across the United States, Russia, France, and Italy, and pages of clear-eyed scholarship, Rampersad's *The Life of Langston Hughes, Vol. I, 1902–1941: I, Too, Sing America* and *The Life of Langston Hughes, Vol. II, 1941–1967: I Dream a World* are altogether dull. Rampersad casts Hughes as a classy, very normal, Duke Ellington of poetry: no demons, no skeletons, no hang-ups. My Hughes research paper had about as much insight as an encyclopedia entry. I wrote it, made, I think, an A, and moved on to your typical high school fantasies of sexual and athletic conquests. Nothing I read or wrote made me think I, the bastard, undereducated son of the South could be a poet. A black poet was respectable, prolific, light-skinned. Years later, after I'd discovered Knight and the boundless galaxy of poetry, I learned there was much unsaid about Hughes. As Darryl Pinckney wrote in his 1989 *New York Review of Books* piece, Rampersad said too little "about Hughes's small hours and who, if anyone, was with him when he closed his door against the world." By the time I learned there was more than meets the eye to Hughes, I was already chasing Knight—my mirror poet. I was certainly more Kinbote than Rampersad in my pursuit. I sidestepped research for guesswork; I was reading between the lines of photographs, interviews, letters, maps, scraps of details. Online I found the *Callaloo* special 1996 issue section featuring Knight's poems, letters, and an interview editor Charles Rowell conducted with Knight in Indianapolis between mid-1975 and late 1978. Jean Anaporte-Easton's essay, "Etheridge Knight: Poet and Prisoner—An Introduction" provides thorough and thoughtful preamble. I heard she was working on a book, but that book has not yet materialized. The most comprehensive Knight study to date is Michael S. Collins's *Understanding Etheridge Knight*, published by the University of South Carolina Press in 2012. Collins offers a straightforward examination of Knight's life and poems. Who can define "distant influence"?

The NUCLEOLUS is an essential, inexplicable, unadulterated self: the lover personality, the trickster personality, the intuitive personality, the multiple true names in a cell. The NUCLEUS is a sphere of identity (southerner, black, son, male, convict, poet) around the nucleolus. Identity drifts over the mind and body in a cell.

LOVES resemble lightning rods, asymmetrical tracks, slanted crosses, bone-tired bones, prostrate limbs. As in the old footpath of a first love; the barely discernible trail of a crush. It is easier to love without speaking. Orpheus dragged long silences around with him.

When I traveled to the smallest part of my body, I found CYTOPLASMIC SPACE. I am often a STRANGER to myself. It is in the restless wrestling to make a song out of despair that the HOPE begins to wheel and vibrate.

FAMILY is a vast system of interconnected members, enfolded and convoluted sacks of nurture and/or trouble located in the selves' cytoplasm. Some family smoothly transports nostalgia, hope, esteem, love, and other positive materials through the cell. Some family is a hive, a rough patch, an outbreak that gives the appearance of several chips on a shrugging shoulder. A flattened, layered, sac-like stack of FEARS hovers near the heart of things. FUCKUPS move fear to other regions. Regarding love and addiction: it's not that the highs last, it's that one wants them to end so nostalgia can root itself in the future. Memory is more enduring than event.

The influence of TEACHERS, the influence of FRIENDS who become teachers, as in relationships that convert the energy found in ignorance to the energy found in acquaintance, benevolence, fellowship. I'm still mulling the dimensions of a "cell." Biology is chance. Biography is chance.

AT WHAT POINT WAS THE FINAL FATE INITIALLY SPECIFIED?

Fate is still waiting to be specified.

Fate is still waiting to be sealed. I'm thinking of meanings in a word like "cell." The cells adrift in a self adrift in a cell; the self between the cells that make us and the cells we make; the space around the nucleus of sensibility; the membrane around "The Idea of Ancestry." Taped to the wall of Knight's cell were the pictures of serenity, kinship, fellowship. I imagine the black faces of friends and teachers taped to the wall of his cell: a black face beneath a black hand raised like a visor over a squint; I'm imagining a black face adrift above a housedress, black faces gathered beneath an astronomical sky, black faces around a card table, a black face framed by a barn door. A lucky future biographer will need to speak to whomever is still alive among those 47 black faces, and if lucky, retrieve each of the 47 pictures taped to the wall of the cell.

LINE 5: ACROSS THE SPACE

In fiction, the coming-of-age story is called a *Bildungsroman*. Essentially, a young protagonist has the sort of experiences that make him or her grow up: Mark Twain's *Adventures of Huckleberry Finn*, Harper Lee's *To Kill a Mockingbird*, Toni Cade Bambara's *Gorilla, My Love*, Ralph Ellison's *Invisible Man*. This sort of story is also popular in memoir, but there's no comparable notion in poetry. How does someone become a poet? It may be that poets come of age with their heads down. Down in books. I, for example, didn't go off to war or to prison, I went off to all the libraries and bookstores in my hometown. I went off to college on a basketball scholarship. One day early in my freshman year I went off to my English professor's office to meet the poet Fran Quinn. I don't even recall whether he gave a public reading during his visit. I remember he didn't read from a book. He read to me from papers bound by a binder clip and I read to him the best of the altogether terrible poems I'd shown no one but my professor. My coming-of-age story begins unheroically with me on a college bunk reading "The Idea of Ancestry" in a literature textbook. It may be that poets come of age staring across space as the speaker does in that poem. I read the poet's biography: a black man from Mississippi, a prisoner who became a poet. I didn't know anything then about "constructed speakers" in poems; I believed the "I" of the poem was Etheridge Knight. I recognized him. Fran Quinn must have offered some encouragement after reading my poems, but what I remember is that he wanted to talk about reading. When he asked what living poets I liked, I mentioned Etheridge Knight. Fran broke into a surprised smile. "Well," he said, "Etheridge Knight happens to be a dear friend of mine." Then, though he'd only just met me, he invited me to Indianapolis to meet Knight.

In the opening scene of "The Idea of Ancestry," Etheridge Knight stares at the faces on his cell wall. He has a revelation. He decides to shape his thoughts of these faces into a poem. It may be that a poet cannot *mature* until experiencing a bit of life. This may explain why the Yale Series of Younger Poets has no clear age cap. "Younger" is synonymous with "emerging," "undiscovered." And Knight, who was incarcerated at twenty-eight, seems to offer a perfect example of the true

Bildungsroman Poem. But instead of coming of age it is something like Coming of Late Age, Coming of Maturity. This notion is not far from William Wordsworth's assertion in his Preface to *Lyrical Ballads* that poetry "takes its origin from emotion recollected in tranquillity." Poetry, this suggests, does not take its origin from action—the sort of action that makes for great coming-of-age stories. No poet's origin story is contained in a single experience. "The Idea of Ancestry" suits Etheridge Knight's story of becoming a poet. It's the story I want to challenge.

It's one of his best-known poems. And according to Knight, it is among the first poems he wrote. "I had just been in the hole some thirty or forty days and that poem came," he said in the *Callaloo* interview. This is perhaps a perverse version of Wordsworth's tranquillity. Social scientists and human rights activists have long detailed the trauma of solitary confinement for just a few hours, not to mention thirty or forty days. Knight frames it as the catalyst for his poem. He does not mention solitary confinement in the poem, however. One imagines a cell where his pictures regularly hang. He's not under particular duress. The faces prompt his recollection. He begins with a catalogue of family members, and then in the second section brings in metaphor, imagery, and vernacular flavor. The poem is maturely crafted. He's got two sections. He employs his famous slashes. He knows someone is going to *read* the thing he's written. He liked to say he became a poet in prison. His first book was titled *Poems from Prison*. For much of his career he introduced himself to audiences with the same two sentences: "I died in Korea from a shrapnel wound and narcotics resurrected me. I died in 1960 from a prison sentence and poetry brought me back to life." His origin story casts him in the company of political prisoners, outlaws, artists, and bluesmen who'd weathered prison. For Knight, Malcolm X was first among them. In fact, four poems in his debut are for or about Malcolm X: "Portrait of Malcolm X," "For Malcolm, a Year After," "It Was a Funky Deal," and "The Sun Came." Many poems in the book consider how or whether one can be rehabilitated while remaining a rebel. There is Malcolm X, the spiritual rebel. There is Hard Rock, the rebel "bad nigger." There is the sage spirit of "He Sees through Stone" and the broken spirit in "For Freckle-Faced Gerald."

Knight believed he came of age as a poet when in prison, because it was there he came to understand his calling: "I began to define myself as a poet in prison," he told Charles Rowell in the *Callaloo* interview.

> Before then, I had been writing toasts about incidents, about things in the neighborhood. I would make them up. When I would go to jail, guys would come around and say, "Hey, Knight"—this was especially after supper, like a social hour in jail—"Hey, Knight, tell us a tale."

"Hard Rock Returns to Prison from the Hospital for the Criminal Insane" has the flavor of one of those tales. Hard Rock, like Shine, Stagger Lee, and John Henry, the black folk heroes, "was 'known not to take no shit from nobody.'" Knight's gifts as a storyteller are evident throughout his poetry. What kind of storyteller was he before prison? Did he tell stories to fellow soldiers during the war? Did he promise tall tales and toasts to drivers when he hitchhiked across the country? We get none of those tales. Instead Knight displays his uncanny gifts in a poem like "Hard Rock Returns to Prison from the Hospital for the Criminal Insane." Knight offers his flair for imagery: "Split purple lips, lumped ears, welts above / [Hard Rock's] yellow eyes, and one long scar that cut / Across his temple and plowed through a thick / Canopy of kinky hair."

Knight's diction is seasoned with vernacular music: "A hillbilly called him a black son of a bitch / And didn't lose his teeth, a screw who knew Hard Rock / From before shook him down and barked in his face. / And Hard Rock did *nothing*. Just grinned and looked silly." What makes the poem noteworthy is its ending move from the tall-tale mode to more poetic language: "He had been our Destroyer, the doer of things / We dreamed of doing but could not bring ourselves to do." The lines echo Ossie Davis's eulogy for Malcolm X: "And if you knew him, you would know why we must honor him: Malcolm was our manhood, our living, black manhood!" "Hard Rock Returns to Prison from the Hospital for the Criminal Insane," like many of the poems in Knight's debut, explores masculinity and blackness. The poem is an example of Knight's transformation from toaster-storyteller to griot-orator. This could be said for the whole of *Poems from Prison*. Knight sold himself as both selves: the artist with a critique of incarceration as well as the artist with an endorsement of rehabilitation.

"The Idea of Ancestry" is the only poem in the debut that hints at the period before Knight "began to define himself as a poet." According to Anaporte-Easton's "Etheridge Knight: Poet and Prisoner," Knight "had no memory of his first few months at the prison. But then, realizing prison could destroy him, he pulled himself together, read voraciously, and committed himself to poetry." The characterization fits with Knight's conversion story. Still, much is glossed over in the moment Knight realizes prison could destroy him and turns to poetry. And why poetry? He'd published three stories in the *Negro Digest*: "Reaching Is His Rule" in the December 1965 issue, "My Father, My Bottom, My Fleas" in the August 1966 issue, and "On the Next Train South" in the June 1967 issue. The stories are short, never more than eight or so pages featuring a single protagonist and third-person-limited narration, but they display Knight's talent for scene and characterization. In "Reaching Is His Rule" a ten-year-old boy named Prather Davis follows his mother out of a police station. While the policemen look indifferently upon the distressed and arrested, Prather is ashamed to feel his mother's hand cuffed around his. Knight describes the feeling in the boy's throat: "He choked from it," because "his brother, A. Philip, who had been named after that big Pullman Porter man and who had come home this summer from Fisk with a beard," had taken Prather to a civil rights demonstration. Prather had been lost in the police-versus-protesters commotion. The whereabouts of A. Philip were unknown. Prather waited at the police station until his mother retrieved him. Knight's short story reads like a vignette in a young adult novel, a bildungsroman whose primary audience is around the age of the protagonist. Both of the short stories I read feature trains and an atmosphere of loneliness. In "On the Next Train South," the main character, Russell Payton, throws a clod of dirt at a dragonfly he addresses as "Mr. Snake

Doctor, Sir." Later, when Russell awaits a woman arriving from Chicago by train, to attend the funeral of his friend, Knight writes, "From beyond the ticket window the cricket-like clicks of the telegraph keys unsettled the quietness." The short stories reveal a direct and musical prose. A similar style is present in his prison journals. In his 1963 prison notebook he writes: "I read that the seven most beautiful words in the English language are: Lure, Allure, Lilt, Flotilla, Downy, Moon, and Love."

The early notebooks display the intimacy of someone writing for himself; the fiction a few years later suggests Knight is blending his personal biography with blues motifs. Though Knight's poems withhold large portions of his life before prison, they are unique in their emotional/

confessional divulgences. The best poems in *Poems from Prison* do not
rely on rhetoric and abstractions about racism. They are full of black,
particular faces. Knight embraced the Black Arts movement—Black
Power, Black Beauty—happening outside of prison. Upon the arrival
of some new inmates, for example, he writes in a 1968 prison newspaper
column:

> Through the back gate in the south wall the young ones came. Chained
> and manacled like a coffle of slaves, they hobbled along in their leg irons.
> They wore their hair long, flaring out from their heads and tikis and other
> charms hung around their necks.

Knight became more and more of a spokesman for Black liberation toward the end of his incarceration. In January 1968, eleven months before his parole, he'd contributed (as did Robert Hayden, Gwendolyn
Brooks, Don L. Lee, Margaret Walker, and a young Alice Walker) to
the *Negro Digest* symposium "Literary Lions and Values"—Richard
Wright being the Leading Lion. In Knight's piece, he writes:

> Unless the Black Artist establishes a "black aesthetic" he will have no fu-
> ture at all. To accept the white aesthetic is to accept and validate a society
> that will not allow him to live. . . . Further, he must hasten his own dis-
> solution as an individual (in the Western sense)—painful though the
> process may be, having been breast-fed on the poison of "individual ex-
> perience."

It's hard to believe Knight held this view when he began writing, con-
sidering his elegy "To Dinah Washington," the first poem he published.
It had appeared three years earlier, in the July 1965 issue of the *Negro
Digest*, and begins: "I have heard your voice floating, royal and real, /
Across the dusky neighborhoods," and ends elegiacally:

Wherever a man is without a warm woman,
Or a woman without her muscled man,
The eternal song is sung.

Some say you're sleeping,
But I say you're singing.

Unforgettable Queen.

When the poem appeared it garnered the attention of poet Gwendolyn Brooks and editor Dudley Randall. Randall published *Poems from Prison* (1968) as well as Knight's second book, *Belly Song* (1973). Randall was a poetry promoter and soldier, a sort of literary Berry Gordy. He'd founded Broadside Press in Detroit in 1965, and among the more than 400 poets he went on to publish were the era's most prominent talents: Margaret Walker, Melvin Tolson, Gwendolyn Brooks, and Robert Hayden. Hayden and Randall were close friends. Randall was among the first to publish many of the young Black Arts poets, among them Nikki Giovanni, Sonia Sanchez, and Don L. Lee, aka Haki Madhubuti. (He also published Audre Lorde's second book at Gwendolyn Brooks's urging.) Knight would have been very willing to talk to anyone in a position to publish or publicize his poems. In the *Callaloo* interview Knight tells Rowell: "They would come down to the 'joint' and see me. They would give me advice, and I would give them advice." According to Randall they workshopped Knight's poems in "a small room reserved for consultations with death row inmates, with iron doors slamming and prisoners shouting in the background."

If they influenced or advised him in the composition of "The Idea of Ancestry," he never said so. But it's not difficult to imagine the wise counsel of Gwendolyn Brooks, mother to every young black poet to come her way. In her preface to *Poems from Prison*, Gwendolyn Brooks contradicts the despair in "To Make a Poem in Prison." Knight spends more than half the poem telling us the difficulties of making poetry where "the air lends itself not to the singer," while Brooks directly asserts, "There is air in these poems." Knight's poem claims "soft words are rare," while Brooks writes, "There are centers of controlled softness too." Brooks declares the poems are more than poems from or about prison. In doing so she declares Knight is more than a prison poet. "The Idea of Ancestry" accounts for both Knight's self-image and Brooks's image of him. It's not an optimistic poem. Nor is it a critique of the prison system in any political sense. It displays the combination of vulnerability and longing that distinguished Knight. Brooks encouraged the centers of softness while Knight seemed to have stared at the walls. This is the end of "The Sun on Those," the first poem in the first book of Jimmy Santiago Baca, another poet who discovered poetry in prison: "Walls and fences cannot take me away from who I am, and I / know, as the tree knows, where I come from, who is my father." In Baca's poem, prison is neither a place of origins nor a place that can hinder his origins. In Knight's poem, "walls and fences" prevent his connectedness to his past. Walls frame his coming of age.

Knight never quite gets beyond the walls of the cell. On the one hand, he continues the work he began as a prison advocate. He edited *Black Voices from Prison*, an anthology of writing by incarcerated men. An introduction by Italian sociologist Roberto Giammanco and writing by ten inmates are framed—almost overshadowed—by Knight's preface, prose, and selections from his *Poems from Prison*. "For Freckle-Faced Gerald" and "Hard Rock" bookend "The Innocents," a prose section that offers commentary on prison's victims and rebels. Knight tells the story of Donald Peck, a Gerald-like inmate, who was victimized "not only because of his innocence, but also because of his youth, good looks, and timidity." And of J.W. Icewater Prewitt, a Hard Rock–like figure who was ready "to fight anybody despite his small size and youth." The title *Black Voices from Prison* echoes *Poems from Prison* and shows how Knight was, at least for a moment, like Malcolm X: a model of willful transformation, a model of rehabilitation and rediscovery.

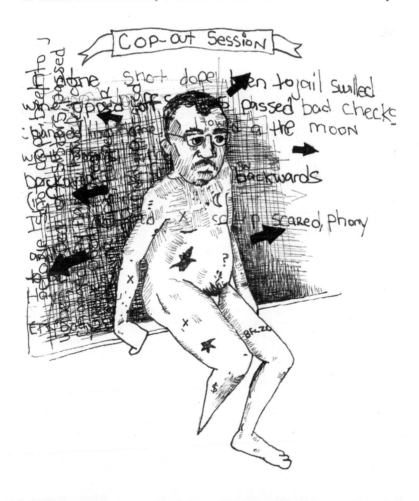

On the other hand, he returned to the habits that landed him in prison. In a 1970 letter to Dudley Randall he confesses, "I'm hooked—have been for eight months now. Sonia and I are separated—I've blown the one/great/love of my life." He alludes to "To Make a Poem in Prison," writing, "I don't know how to run it down without sounding melodramatic and full of self pity. But pity is not for the poet; truth and love are . . . I stopped writing almost altogether (I couldn't be dishonest enough to write for Black people while living such an unblack life)." He can be seen decked in all black with a militant tilt to his beret in 1972, among the Black Arts poets at the University of Dayton to celebrate the centennial of the birth of Paul Laurence Dunbar. Sonia Sanchez reads as well. Knight is drunk or high, rambling at length about Paul Laurence Dunbar, honky applause, and the Wright brothers before reading his poems. He hits all his usual biographical notes with slurred intensity. "I didn't go to college as all of you did, I went to prison instead," tangentially distinguishing the larger prison he found after getting out of prison. "Suppose I was black and a woman and a homosexual and I was in prison," he says, to the audience's laughter, before explicating and then magnificently reading "For Freckle-Faced Gerald." When he reads what he says are poems he wrote after getting out of prison, he does not mention his relapse with the law. A year before the Dunbar centennial reading, he'd been in Connecticut's Bridgeport Correctional Center for possession of heroin. The following excerpt highlights how quickly he slid back into his prison-writer persona.

> Sounds carom down the corridors, reverberating and magnifying. You can lie in your cell and dig the whole joint with your ears: a man urinating,

the toilet flushing, a man screaming in his sleep, another coughing and snoring and always—keys jingling and bells ringing, steel doors slamming. Jail sounds, sounds of ice.

Knight ends his Dunbar reading with what he calls a fun poem written since he was in jail: "The Nixon Flu." He applies his storyteller's bravado to a humorous but thin political sketch. Meanwhile the letters he sent to writers, friends, editors, and associates revealed what Brooks had called his "centers of controlled softness." "Control" because there were dimensions of "management" (hustle) at work. He sent the excerpt above to seven different advocates and one literary journal. He struck both the pensive, sober inmate of "The Idea of Ancestry" and the "confused, fucked up, scared, phony" of "Cop-Out Session," one of the shoddier poems of *Poems from Prison*. But there was "softness" because as the excerpt shows, Knight was a writer in prison, not a prison writer. He was a witness.

The first time I read "The Idea of Ancestry," it was the closest thing I'd seen to a poem about coming of age as a poet. The poet was a black man who'd "kicked it with the kinfolks" in the "hills and red gullies of mississippi." I believed the story Knight told me. He had some experiences and recollected them in the relative tranquillity of prison. The poem is about that experience. No poet's origin story is contained in a single experience. Who was Knight before prison? What girl broke his heart, what songs did he sing, what poems did he read? I have thought the same thought about Black Arts poets Amiri Baraka and Sonia Sanchez: Who were they before they became Black Arts poets? What happens when a young black poet discovers poetry before he or she discovers politics? I can't imagine half of it.

When Fran Quinn invited me to meet Etheridge Knight, I could not imagine the poet anywhere except prison. I thought he was a prison poet. My mother worked for the South Carolina Department of Corrections. Would she allow me to visit an ex-convict in Indianapolis? I would have had to go against her wishes. Nine hours through South Carolina, Tennessee, and Kentucky with little more than my terrible poems. I became a poet with my head down. In a book. In another life, the visit would be at the heart of my coming-of-age story. Had I gone I would have learned Knight was captive now to his own broken, deteriorating body. He'd been in a terrible car accident; he was also dying from cancer. I may have sat with the circle of people around him: his mother, Belzora, his poetry comrades, his former and current lovers, and his students. These people were not drawn to his poems from prison, they were drawn to him. My coming-of-age story is about a road I did not take. I was not dreaming of life as a poet before I became a poet. Maybe we can say the same of Knight. I never talked to my parents about poetry. I never mentioned the day, in my freshman year of college, that I met Fran Quinn, a man who made his life as a poet. He gave me his phone number after doing little more than reading my poems. He insisted I visit him and Etheridge in Indiana during the Christmas holidays. I said okay, but when the holidays neared, I backed out. I was afraid. I promised Fran I'd visit during the coming summer or maybe during spring break. It was a promise I never got to break. That March Etheridge Knight passed away.

LINE 7: I AM ALL OF THEM

KNIGHT'S VEST OF SELVES

Etheridge / Mr. Knight	Junior / Mr.K
jives / lectures	works / sleeps
without / with	above / beneath
ignoring / visions	fields / skies
Feelings of / of senseless	blacker than / lighter than
heaviness / emptiness	the skin / the blood
around / inside	around / inside
his bones / his heart	his bones / his heart

LINE 8: I AM A THIEF

PORTRAIT OF ETHERIDGE KNIGHT

IN THE STYLE OF A CRIME REPORT

CRIME/INCIDENT REPORT

	RELATED REPORTS	ADDITIONAL OFFENSES LISTED IN NARRATIVE	CASE NUMBER		
C R I M E	Yes, you should run down Knight's criminal records. Readers will be especially interested in the circumstances under which he first was imprisoned.	During a visit home to Mississippi Knight claims to have broken into the office of a doctor, possibly a dentist, to acquire drugs. It is unclear what drugs Knight obtained. The following is a reconfigured dramatization of events.	There is a number between every number.		

CODE SECTION AND DESCRIPTION (ONE INCIDENT ONLY)	MONTH	DAY OF THE WEEK	YEAR	TIME
When the store clerk wasn't looking, Knight pulled cash from the register. The judge gave him eight years upstate.	Therefore we can assume this happens between months of summer.	On the previous day the clan gathers for a picnic.	They wear denim and cotton in the style of rural black people in the 1950s.	Their laughter, chatter, multi-scented smoke, and funk burns through the edges of the day.

LOCATION OF INCIDENT (OR ADDRESS)	CITY
The sun sets late in Memphis. You can get there from Corinth, Mississippi, as late as ten o'clock and still have to wait for the darkness.	

VICTIM'S NAME	RESIDENCE ADDRESS CITY
We are not sure whether Knight knew the doctor's name. He was called Doctor, whether he was a physician or a dentist.	STATE ZIP In the cell's darkness, the code of ancestry breaks.

VICTIM

SEE RACE CODE LEGEND ON TOP OF BACK PAGE	RACE	SEX	DATE OF BIRTH	RELATION TO VICTIM/SUSPECT
In the darkness the cells break.	He was called Doctor whether he was black or white.	He had a homely wife and a shy nurse. His wife may have also been his nurse.	There are root doctors in foreign countries who believe a man's whole life can be mapped according to his birthday.	Etheridge had come across a witch doctor in a bar in LA. A guy with a pink scar running like a seam, a dividing line, down the middle of his face. When he asked Etheridge where he was from, Etheridge took it to mean if he could find his way to Mississippi, he'd find his way.

PROPERTY

ARTICLE NAME	STOLEN / RETRIEVED	IDENTIFICATION NUMBERS	BRAND/MAKE OR MANUFACTURER	MISCELLANEOUS DESCRIPTION	VALUE
Diacetylmorphine	is stolen.	Because pleasure is a form of metamorphosis, a man doses off dreaming of Mississippi and wakes as a horse at a barbed fence.			
Points aiming to puncture skin	are retrieved.	Insulin and tuberculin syringes, subcutaneous injectors, hypodermic needles ranging from ½ an inch to 3 inches.			
Cures for depression	are stolen.	I am embarrassed by how bad I am with money. I don't know what to do with it or what to do without it. I believe the high is not symbolic, it is not dialectic. It is a form of metamorphosis.			
Cures for joy	are stolen and retrieved.	The only thing stronger than joy is my hunger for joy. It's a fact, the bones of a horse last longer than the horse.			

SUSPECT

HAIR LENGTH/TYPE	HAIR STYLE	FACIAL HAIR	COMPLEXION	GENERAL APPEARANCE	DEMEANOR	SPEECH	VOICE

Bald Afro Braided Collar Shoulder Processed Thinning Ponytail Coarse Wavy Greasy Thick Short Neck Wig Clean-shaven with acne. Sideburned and dark. Disguised, disgusting, good-looking, unkempt. Sometimes the suspect is angry and then inhumanly calm. The suspect may be disorganized. His lisp may be muffled or raspy. He may speak with a Negro accent. He may be lost in thought.

No one was arrested that day. A boy questioned just outside Memphis claimed he saw a dark gray horse trotting across his front yard that night.

LINE 9: I HAVE AT ONE TIME
OR ANOTHER BEEN IN LOVE

LINE 11: I AM NOW IN LOVE

AS YOU LEAVE ME
BY ETHERIDGE KNIGHT

Shiny record albums scattered over
the living room floor, reflecting light
from the lamp, sharp reflections that hurt
my eyes as I watch you, squatting among the platters,
the beer foam making mustaches on your lips.

And, too,
the shadows on your cheeks from your long lashes
fascinate me—almost as much as the dimples
in your cheeks, your arms, and your legs.

You
hum along with Mathis—how you love Mathis!
with his burnished hair and quicksilver voice that dances
among the stars and whirls through canyons
like windblown snow, sometimes I think that Mathis
could take you from me if you could be complete
without me. I glance at my watch. It is now time.

You rise,

silently, and to the bedroom and the paint;

on the lips red, on the eyes black,

and I lean in the doorway and smoke, and see you

grow old before my eyes, and smoke. why do you

chatter while you dress? and smile when you grab

your large leather purse? don't you know that when you

leave me I walk to the window and watch you? and light

a reefer as I watch you? and I die as I watch you

disappear in the dark streets

to whistle and smile at the johns.

POET DYING AT THE WINDOW
BY TERRANCE HAYES

I have a goddamn for every blade

of snow. You're not even to the road

before it's clinging to your coat.

Said I wouldn't write anymore

about matters of the heart,

so I'm writing about the snow—

God's cryogenic rain; cold trick/le

of repetition falling quietly as ghosts.

Is this what Etheridge meant?
Walls blacker than a throat;
Poet dying at the window;
Flakes/ covering your tracks as you go.

In my first book is "Poet Dying at the Window," which is essentially an imitation of Etheridge Knight's "As You Leave Me." I wrote the poem in my early twenties when I thought it was proper, even flattering, to paint a woman as an object of desire. At the time, all a beautiful woman was to me was something to be desired from a distance. My own first poems were little more than love notes to my middle school and then high school and then college crushes. The word *crush* brings to mind rumpled paper stuffed into rumpled envelopes stuffed into my pants pockets and then stuffed quickly into the palms of the girls or the friends of the girls crushing my heart. I can't remember a single tender *yes*. The heaving and sighing, rising and falling was good decent practice for my boy's heart, then my young man's heart, then my married man's heart. Practice, a verb synonymous with training, became a noun synonymous with *habit*, praxis. In any case, the subject and practice of desire was the common topic of conversation among my pals—be they athletes or writers. With my pal Renegade, a fellow baller and poet, desire was the topic we carried from workouts to workshops. Often we bounced ideas about the nature of desire in Etheridge Knight's poetry. We battled over "As You Leave Me," in particular. Renegade argued the woman in the poem was very likely a prostitute. My take was simply that I didn't know. I didn't think so, but I didn't know. Renegade, being just about a decade older than I am, has always assumed the wise stance of my worldly older brother with regards to the poem and just about everything else in the world. He reasoned she was probably not his "beloved" because Knight called the men she whistles at "johns." Maybe the men she encounters are johns but that doesn't make her a hooker by default. And anyway is any woman ballsy enough to whistle at strange men necessarily a hooker?

I've become less and less interested in her vocation over the years, but I remain very interested (just as the speaker is) in the woman moving through the room like a muse or apparition. We get to watch the watcher watching her. The poem's primary refrain is this watching: "my eyes as I watch you," "my watch," "don't you know that when you / leave me I walk to the window and watch you? and light / a reefer as I watch you? and die as I watch you." All through literature we find lovers watching and waiting on balconies and docks, at bus stops and restaurants and windows. Act 2, scene 2 of *Romeo and Juliet* ends with Juliet's promise to wait: "Good night, good night! Parting is such sweet sorrow / That I shall say good night till it be morrow." In *A Lover's Discourse: Fragments*, Roland Barthes tells us, "The lover's fatal identity is precisely: *I am the one who waits*." The one who waits is always lonely. The lover leaves, and the lover left writes to fill the ache. If that sounds too romantic, we could say Knight's poem captures the real time of the situation.

In the preface to her essay collection *On Longing*, Susan Stewart defines narrative as "a structure of desire, a structure that both invents and distances its object." It's a definition suggestive of desire's relation to storytelling. Desire gives shape to what has, and to what might have, happened.

When Stewart invokes structure, she is suggesting narrative itself has a shape. This isn't news. The nineteenth-century German writer Gustav Freytag illustrated this shape in a diagram that has come to be known as Freytag's Triangle.

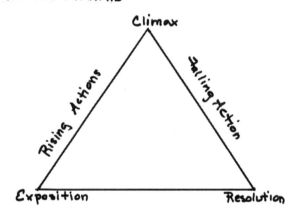

We learned the parts in high school English class: Exposition, Rising Action, Climax, Falling Action, and Resolution/Denouement. I like to think of the structure as a line with a peak in the middle of it. The peak is the *point* of the story.

"As You Leave Me" is of interest in this context, because Knight manages to suggest a narrative arc while omitting large parts of the story. It's those omissions that fuel my debates with Renegade. It's those omissions that make the poem such terrific theater. Knight concentrates on a particular *slope* of the narrative triangle, instead of the exposition and climax. He clips all the ordinary time around the moment: the courtship, the coitus. His poem narrates the moment of falling action just after the lover's literal, figurative, and structural climax and just before one lover's exit. We don't know whether it's nearer to midnight or dawn, but behind or beneath the poem is a poetic form known as the aubade, a song or poem about lovers separating at dawn. In its strictest sense, the aubade is sung to "a sleeping woman" by her detached, departing suitor. Imagine him grabbing his coat and hat (his cowboy hat, fedora, helmet, or baseball cap depending on the genre and era) and tiptoeing out the door. In "As You Leave Me," it's the woman —cool, mysterious, the strong silent type—who is leaving the suitor. "I think that Mathis / could take you from me if you could be complete / without me," the watcher says while she prepares to depart. Here I can hear Renegade saying that's evidence she's a prostitute: object of his desires. I can hear myself saying one who focuses on the woman's occupation makes the same error as the watcher who presumes to know and control her. It's not her *occupation* but what *occupies* her that matters. What occupies her, at least in the moment the poem captures, is not the watcher. He can't make her do anything: he can't make her stay or speak to him. He only has the power of a voyeur. A voyeur's only power is longing.

Don't get me wrong: longing is hella powerful. Some years ago I traveled to Brussels, to a writing residency, in search of writerly solitude.

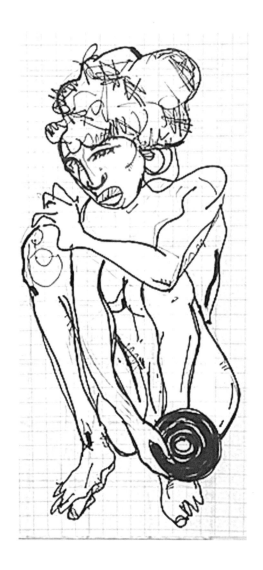

To my surprise, that solitude collapsed too often into longing. Longing overwhelmed much of my writing there. Each morning I was distracted by the beautiful baristas working in a tiny café near my flat. Once I spied a lovely redheaded cashier in a loose skirt lift her naked foot to show a lovely co-worker her brightly painted toenails. I spied her Achilles'

heel, her ankle, her calf. Like Knight's watchman, I watched her move through clouds of chatter with no mind on my attentions. There often was an old man with a hound and an ornate cane waiting beside him in the café. A fellow watcher. His nostrils flared ever so slightly when one of the waitresses leaned over him. Mr. Achilles, I said under my breath.

Stewart's definition of narrative suggests desire animates all stories. She makes me wonder about a comparable definition of lyric. Is lyric not also "a structure of desire"; is lyric not also "a structure that both invents and distances its object"? I think yes, but obviously lyric and narrative have very different shapes. If stories are generally triangular, lyric is circular. Lyric, like longing, has no discernible beginning, middle, and end—it's always happening in the now. The speaker is in love with "47 black faces" on a "gray stone wall." He loves the folks who love him enough to send photos. It's easy to bypass the romantic longing in the poem when it is couched in family. The speaker pines for love. Actually, let's dispense with the thin line separating the speaker of the poem and Knight the poet. I will sometimes call the "I" in these poems a "speaker," but really it ain't nobody but Knight. Or a somebody so much like Knight he could be his shadow. When Knight writes, "I have at one time or another been in love," my response is: "No shit, Brother!" Knight was married twice by official law and married three times by what they used to call "common law." From the year of his release until his death in 1991, he introduced himself to audiences as a prison poet, but he could have just as easily introduced himself as a lovelorn poet, a heartsick, heartbroken, heartaching poet. We see it in "The Idea of Ancestry." We see it in "As You Leave Me" and in many

48

of the poems he wrote after prison. But "As You Leave Me" is not actually a love poem. That, I think, was part of my debate with Renegade. It's a poem of longing, a poem of the postcoital blues. It's really in his second book, *Belly Song*, that we begin to sense the true resonances of "I have at one time or another been in love." The book is dedicated to his mother and his "woman, Mary Ellen McAnally" but the introduction is based on an actual letter Knight wrote to Sonia Sanchez just before getting out of prison.

The November 7, 1968, letter to Sanchez, sent to a San Francisco address, begins:

> Baby—
>
> Yeah, well, I made it. No hip-hip-hoorays, but I do feel good about it—not *grateful*, but good. At least I'll be with my woman and children in the larger outside prison. Each day we move closer, and each day I love you more—if that's possible.

Belly Song is published five years later with an introduction also dated November 7, 1968, but beginning:

> Lady—
>
> Yeah, well, I made it. Parole. No hip-hip-hoorays, but I do feel good about it—not *grateful*, but good. At least I'll be with my woman and children in the larger outside prison. Each day we move closer, Lady.

Sonia Sanchez had been introduced to his poetry by Dudley Randall, who was also Sanchez's editor. Maybe Randall and Gwendolyn Brooks encouraged Sanchez to write to Knight. Randall was particularly interested in their courtship. "Talked with Sonia long distance the other night," he wrote in a September 1968 letter to Knight. "She said to give you her love, but you know all that's going on, as she writes you every day." Then parenthetically Randall exclaims: "(Man, how do you do it? And she's never even seen you!)." Knight was paroled a month later and married Sanchez before the year passed. (Those must have been amazing letters.) Within two years, they were divorced. I have come across no letters or in-depth interviews wherein Sanchez talks about Knight. I once told myself if I could interview her, I'd have enough for a Knight biography. But she doesn't talk about those years. Sanchez already had twin baby boys and a daughter when she and Knight married. You can imagine the sort of stepfather and husband a recently paroled, former and soon-to-be drug addict would be. Knight was a junkie cliché. He was violent. He was irresponsible. I heard he once claimed he was taking the boys' dog (maybe it was two dogs) for a walk and sold it for drugs. Nonetheless, Eunice told me Sanchez visited Knight near the end when he was dying twenty years later, in Indianapolis, of lung cancer. All of his loves and ex-loves were at his bedside with his mother, his only true love, according to Eunice. Eunice said Knight and Sanchez were never divorced. It was a Christian marriage but, according to them, a Muslim divorce; Eunice told me: "I don't know about all them white women after Sonia, but I still consider her my sister-in-law."

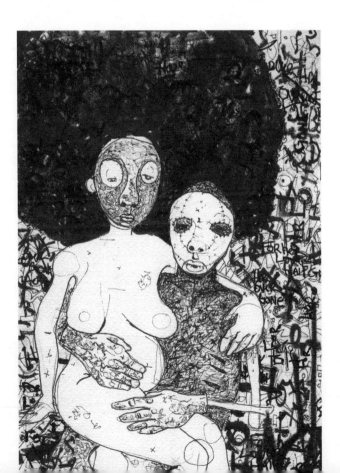

UPON YOUR LEAVING

(FOR SONIA)

BY ETHERIDGE KNIGHT

Night
and in the warm blackness
your woman smell filled the room
and our rivers flowed together. became one
my love's patterns. our sweat / drenched bellies
made flat cracks as we kissed
like sea waves lapping against the shore
rocks rising and rolling and sliding back.

And
your sighs softly calling my name
became love songs child / woman songs
old as a thousand years new as the few
smiles you released like sacred doves. and I
fell asleep, ashamed of my glow of my halo, and
ignoring them who waited below
to take you away when the sun rose . . .

Day
and the sunlight playing in the green leaves
above us fell across your face traced the tears
in your eyes and love patterns in the wet grass.
and as they waited inside in triumphant patience

to take you away I begged you to stay.
"but, etheridge," you said, "i don't know what to do."
and the love patterns shifted and shimmered in your eyes.

And
after they had taken you and gone, the day
turned stark white. bleak. barren like
the nordic landscape. I turned and entered
into the empty house and fell on the floor
laughing. trying to fill the spaces your love had left.
knowing that we would not remain apart long.
our rivers had flowed together.
we are one.
and are strong.

In *Belly Song*, "Upon Your Leaving" is dedicated to Sanchez. The differences between *leave* and *leaving* underscore the contrast with "As You Leave Me." Where we could say "As You Leave Me" has a theatrical staging, "Upon Your Leaving" feels closer to a screenplay—something that plays out on a two-dimensional square. I said earlier, we could dispense with the thin mask of "speaker" in Knight's poems. In "Upon Your Leaving," he does it for us, going so far as to name himself in the poem. A psychiatrist would probably have something to say about his lowercase *e* in "etheridge" juxtaposed with the capital *S* in "Sonia." For me, the explicitness of names underscores the poem's desire for sincerity. It's not a good poem despite its efforts at authenticity.

In "As You Leave Me" the lover *being* left withholds various dimensions of the narrative. In "Upon Your Leaving" the lover *who has been left* intends to disclose everything: "sea waves lapping against the shore," smiles "released like sacred doves," "sunlight playing in the green leaves" across someone's face. As with "As You Leave Me," the speaker is left in an "empty house." But in "Upon Your Leaving" the poet/speaker, is not coolly smoking, he is hysterical:

> after they had taken you and gone, the day
> turned stark white. bleak. barren like
> the nordic landscape. I turned and entered
> into the empty house and fell on the floor
> laughing. trying to fill the spaces your love had left.

The act of love becomes as flat and one-dimensional as a figure on the floor. The poem even proposes a resolution of sorts: "we would not remain apart long." Narrative—the point of the story—is flattened by overstatement. It's the stuff of perfume commercials.

"What you call love was invented by guys like me . . . to sell nylons," Don Draper says in the first episode of *Mad Men*, suggesting that love is constantly worked on, worked over, crafted in all sorts of ways by all sorts of people. Or rather, how susceptible we people who love love can be to the superficial shorthand of love. But it's not simply that the poem needs better details. It's not detail that's needed, but intimacy. I'm talking about the difference between "love's patterns" and love's texture. Texture suggests touch; pattern suggests observation. Where pattern suggests arrangement and design, texture suggests roughness, imperfection—the lover may dream of caressing the smoothest parts of the body, but it's the feel of the pimple, the scar, the goose bumps that the caresser really remembers. There is nothing memorable about perfection, though we often conduct ourselves as if perfection were the aim. Any good adman knows "perfection," or rather the idea of perfection, sells better than subtlety. We have a whole genre of love poems ruined by the lack of subtlety: we call them valentine cards. Who has time for subtlety when all valentines have to be exchanged on a single day. Commerce scorns patience even as it seems to praise authenticity. "Slip the panties right to the side / Ain't got the time to take draws off, on site / Catch a charge I might, beat the box up like Mike," Jay-Z raps to/about Beyoncé in "Drunk in Love." Drunkenness is supposed to suggest an unguarded act, which is supposed to suggest an authentic act. I'm mostly embarrassed for Jay and Bey in ways not unlike my embarrassment for Knight's "Upon Your Leaving." When feeling is overstated, sentimentality is the result. Sometimes when feeling is overstated, pornography is the result. Pornography is a kind of sentimentality, an over-sharing. "A stroke by stroke story of a copulation is exactly as absurd as a chew by chew account of the consumption of a chicken's wing," William Gass tells us in *On Being Blue*.

But let's be honest, pornography is just desire on steroids. It has its place. Sometimes one does not desire subtlety. Returning to Susan Stewart's *On Longing*, pornography is also a narrative genre that "invents and distances its object." Problems certainly arise when the object is in fact a subject. In 2014, the performance artist Deborah de Robertis strolled into the Musée d'Orsay in a dress the color and texture of the frame around Gustave Courbet's *The Origin of the World*. De Robertis then displayed herself for museumgoers, museum staff, and security guards and for at least one camera phone. Rather than disrespecting Courbet, as the museum alleged when they had de Robertis arrested, she highlighted the space between detail and texture, explicit and implicit. Imagination happens in that space. Why, I took her to be asking, is the "real" origin of the world more troubling than a painting of it? Because the art world, like the business world, says *imaginary* pussy is more ideal than *real* pussy. The idea of the object is more manageable than the realities of the subject. The clean, symmetrical pattern of the object is more manageable than the fluid, lyrical texture of the subject. One struggles with the language of intimacy, in part, because it is not a matter of precision but suggestion; not definition but impression. It involves a certain Germanic etymology, a close-to-earth *feeling* versus a more Latinate *sentiment*. It's no coincidence that *feeling* is both a noun and an action.

Now is a good time to tell you of my bewildering adolescent crush on Flannery O'Connor. I had no idea what to do with the feeling. Arousal

is not all about pleasure. Sometimes a little befuddlement is involved, sometimes even a little bit of displeasure. When I'd read O'Connor's short story "The Artificial Nigger" at fifteen, for example, I had no idea why that was the story's title and dared not ask a parent or teacher. I now know it had something to do with the lawn jockeys Mr. Head and his grandson encountered while lost in Atlanta, but for at least a decade after reading the story, it was an uncomfortable curiosity. I came to enjoy the feeling of not knowing the answer. Desire can be like that. In fact, I have come to equate large portions of desire with curiosity. The strange Brussels baristas were desirable because of curiosities I could not solve. Every stranger is a curiosity.

I blame the longing I experienced in Brussels on all the women speaking in strange sensual tongues. One afternoon, my buzzer rang. It was a brief half buzz that made me turn to the door, though I was on the second floor of a locked building, and wait. It buzzed again a bit longer. When I went to the security-camera window, I saw in black and white two beautiful women. "Hello," I said a few times into the intercom, and when they didn't answer, I pushed the button to let them in. Still nothing; they stood confused. Could they be looking for me? Were they looking for one of the writers who'd previously worked in the studio I occupied? "Hello," I called, looking down on them from my second-floor window. One of them, the one whose face I'd seen prominently in the intercom camera, had deep auburn hair pulled back in a ponytail. It was the color of sunlight through a glass of red wine. No bullshit, really, I'm telling you what I thought at the time. They looked up, the one with reddish-black hair and the one with short black hair and said, in relieved unison, something in a language I didn't understand. "English," I begged. "We put something in the wrong mailbox," the one with a merlot-colored ponytail and fitted jeans called up. "I'll have to come down," I said. When I opened the door she only stepped in a foot, saying, "Thank you, thank you," effusively. She opened my mailbox cubbyhole where a lone small key lay. It was quickly retrieved and placed in the appropriate mailbox, and then I was shutting the door again saying, "No problem," to them. For a second the door was opened between us, and glimpsing into that cell, I imagined our tangle.

My standards are not all that high when it comes to longing. Another time as I sat in a Boston bar with a handful of writers, the subject of Flannery O'Connor's beauty, or to be more specific, lack of beauty, arose. *Four-eyed, homely, sickly*—these were the words being dealt before

I admitted, I'd never really *measured* O'Connor's beauty. I hadn't compared her to some abstract idea of beauty. Why would I have thought of anyone but Flannery O'Connor while looking at Flannery O'Connor? She couldn't be unattractive if she was compared to herself. She was neither ugly nor beautiful to me. I stopped short of telling anyone that, as a boy, I'd had something of a crush on her.

FEELING FUCKED UP
BY ETHERIDGE KNIGHT

Lord she's gone done left me done packed / up and split
and I with no way to make her
come back and everywhere the world is bare
bright bone white   crystal sand glistens
dope death dead dying and jiving drove
her away made her take her laughter and her smiles
and her softness and her midnight sighs—

Fuck Coltrane and music and clouds drifting in the sky
fuck the sea and trees and the sky and birds
and alligators and all the animals that roam the earth
fuck marx and mao fuck fidel and nkrumah and
democracy and communism fuck smack and pot
and red ripe tomatoes fuck joseph fuck mary fuck
god jesus and all the disciples fuck fanon nixon
and malcolm fuck the revolution fuck freedom fuck

the whole muthafucking thing
all i want now is my woman back
so my soul can sing

"Feeling Fucked Up" comes right after "Upon Your Leaving" in *Belly Song*. Unlike "Upon Your Leaving, "Feeling Fucked / Up" packs its narrative into six words: "Lord she's gone done left me." Knight's words are pretty much a translation of a sixteenth-century unattributed poem, "Western Wind":

> Western wind when wilt thou blow
> the small rain down can rain
> Christ if my love were in my arms
> and I in my bed again

"Feeling Fucked Up" declares, *All I want is my love in my arms so I can sing*. In both cases, someone is waiting, even if we don't know for whom or why or how long. Reading "Feeling Fucked Up" for the first time in college, I was thrilled to find the word *fuck* repeated so emphatically in a poem. It takes the profane—less complicated minds might associate that with pornography—and recalibrates it to song, to lyrical texture. I couldn't have said that at nineteen, of course. (Instead I filed the feeling—the feeling of "Feeling Fucked Up"—in the vicinity of my Flannery O'Connor feelings.) I got the drift of the first stanza, but mostly rushed through its expository build to the climactic second stanza. The *fuck*s were hotter than the *fuck*s of Ice-T or 2 Live Crew or NWA. Reading the poem now I am actually still thrilled by the *fuck*s. They remind me of something Emily Dickinson writes in a letter rebuffing Otis Lord, an *over*-elderly suitor: "Don't you know that 'No' is the wildest word we consign to Language?" Knight's *fucks* have the same passionate affirmative *No*. They constitute a simultaneous acceptance and repudiation: the blues bravado of saying *fuck time* while longing for more time. In "As You Leave Me," the lover being left enacts a narrative restraint focusing on only the moment of departure. In "Upon Your Leaving," the lover who has been left enacts narrative disclosure that flattens time—flattens the point. "Feeling Fucked Up" contains both the acts displayed in these poems, but more than either, it relies on lyric time. Lyric time is a crisis of narrative—story spiraling out of control. It makes the structure of desire *revolutionary*—with that word's dual connotations of subversiveness and circularity. Desire has a song and story built into it: "I have at one time or another been in love," it says, and I am waiting to be in love again. Desire can make time stand still. Desire can turn time round. Desire can obliterate time; it can in essence fuck it up.

LINE 14: I HAVE
THE SAME NAME

I.

A poetics of liquid requires liquid. Influence is, at it's etymological root, fluid: from medieval Latin *influentia* ("inflow"), from Old French *influence* ("a flow of water"). It was, in the late fourteenth century, an astrological term, "streaming ethereal power from the stars acting upon character or destiny of men." By the mid-fifteenth century it was defined as an "exertion of unseen power over other persons." And we still use it from time to time to mean tangible, immersive, *submersive* power: Under the influence of booze, of drugs. Under the influence of love or greed, of darkness, of hope, of history. What does it mean to be under the influence of poetry?

In her essay collection *When I Was a Child I Read Books*, Marilynne Robinson describes God as "a sphere whose center is everywhere and whose circumference is nowhere," and it seems equally suitable to discuss influence in this way. You sense its presence, but can't exactly say where it begins or ends.

Influence is practical; it does not so much give as give away. This, in fact, is how Robert Bly describes water in "Mourning Pablo Neruda." The poem never actually mentions Neruda. Instead the speaker carries water "to the young willow trees." The poem ends with a meditation on water:

> it goes
> Around us, on the way
> To the Minnesota River,
> To the Mississippi River,
> To the Gulf,
> Always closer
> To where
> It has to be.
> No one lays flowers
> On the grave
> Of water,
> For it is not
> Here,
> It is
> Gone.

Neruda is a poet of water. Poet of surrealism, poet of the historical epic, political poet, erotic poet, poet of feeling, poet of liquid. Bly's poem tells us what we sort of already know about the transparent, protean styles of water. His ending alludes or seems to allude to John Keats's epitaph, "Here lies one whose name was writ in water." A poetics of liquid is certainly influenced by Keats's notion of Negative Capability.

An inability to define Negative Capability is a pretty good definition of negative capability: a reaching after uncertainty, a ripple of reliable ambiguity, a mystery that opens on wave after wave of mystery. Keats did not state it as an explicit poetics when he wrote it about Coleridge in a letter to his brothers, George and Thomas Keats, in 1817, when he was only twenty-two! He meant it as a critique, saying, "With a great poet the sense of Beauty overcomes every other consideration, or rather obliterates all consideration." Negative Capability is either Keats's brilliant premonition about the world to come, our world, or it defines a timeless human state. I realize I am a mystery to myself—how about you? I realize I love mystery. I realize it terrifies me. "At once it struck me, what quality went to form a Man of Achievement especially in Literature & which Shakespeare possessed so enormously," Keats wrote. "I mean Negative Capability, that is when man is capable of being in uncertainties, Mysteries, doubts, without any irritable reaching after fact & reason." It influences our discussion, but it is not quite enough to account for a working poetics of liquid.

A liquid poetics is as much about uncertainty as it is about mutable sensibility: adaptive temperaments and temperatures and forms. I use poetics here as a noun, but isn't it also an adjective? Other genres may be poetic: novels, sunsets too; poetic character, poetic wind. Is the opposite of poetic *prosaic*? If poetic is equal to fluid, is prosaic equal to density: an obfuscating or fundamental mud? Is the opposite of poetics *mechanics* or *mechanistics*: a mathematical, industrial order? Yes. Poetics are not fixed, they are as indescribable and shifty as water. Actually, I don't totally agree when Bly says "water is practical" at the outset of "Mourning Pablo Neruda." Sure, water is necessary, water is nutritious, but water can also be a nuisance. It floods, it steams, it freezes, it rots; "it doesn't care about us, it goes around us"—that's what Bly writes later in the poem. Water has no endgame, no ambition. It is pure procedure. Likewise, one's poetics are most evident in procedure and practice. One's poetics should be liquid.

2.

I haven't mentioned Zygmunt Bauman, born in Poznań, Poland, in 1925. After fifty-plus books wrestling with postmodernity, he devised in *Liquid Modernity* (2000), a means of accounting for "'liquidity' in its application to the form of life currently practiced." In 2003, he published *Liquid Love: On the Frailty of Human Bonds*; in 2005, *Liquid Life*; in 2007, *Liquid Fear* and *Liquid Times: Living in an Age of Uncertainty*. Bauman writes that "the liquid modern man . . . flows through his own life like a tourist, changing places, jobs, spouses, values, and sometimes even more (such as political or sexual orientation . . .)."

He says that "individuals must splice together an unending series of short-term projects and episodes that don't add up to the kind of sequence to which concepts like 'career' and 'progress' could be meaningfully applied. These fragmented lives require individuals to be flexible and adaptable—to be constantly ready and willing to change tactics at short notice, to abandon commitments and loyalties without regret and to pursue opportunities according to their current availability."

Terms like *late modernity* or *postmodernity* don't quite account for *currentness* and all that word connotes: presentness (versus postness or lateness); movement versus stability. Bauman and Bauman-styled sociologists may well say, I'm presenting just the tip of the liquid modernist iceberg, but I wish to use it as a means for understanding poetic influence (and the poetics of influence) in a world simultaneously uncertain and overdetermined.

3.

Cynthia Ozick defines *essay*, in "She: Portrait of the Essay as a Warm Body," thusly: "Like a poem, a genuine essay is made out of language and character and mood and temperament and pluck and chance."

4.

It may not be of interest to you, but when I was young, three or four, in the military housing of Fort Bragg in Fayetteville, North Carolina, where my brother was born, I spent long hours in the basement with a $10 guitar singing and talking to myself. I remember it. A floor above, my mother was also talking to herself. She was only nineteen or twenty. She could have been talking about nothing more than wealth or security or the state in which one need no longer talk needfully to the self. I realize it is confessional to talk at long lengths about one's mother or oneself.

5.

When I encountered Steven Johnson's term *liquid network*, I thought instantly of Bauman's *liquid modernity*. *Where Good Ideas Come From* (2010) is Johnson's book about the nature of creativity. He offers seven patterns of innovation, but I want to mention just three: the adjacent possible pattern, the platform pattern, and the liquid network pattern.

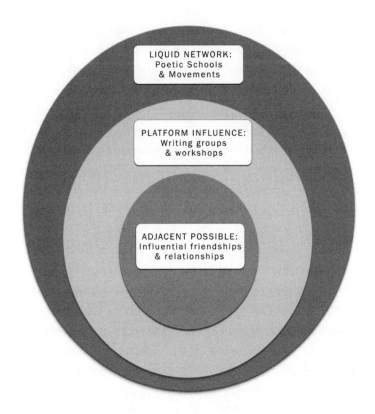

The first innovation pattern, which he calls the "adjacent possible," is where creativity/new ideas are triggered by the influence of intimate bonds. In poetry, we might think of influential friendships like that of Robert Lowell and Elizabeth Bishop, or influential marriages like that of Lowell to each of his three wives, especially his second wife, writer Elizabeth Hardwick—or of mentorships like that of Lowell and his students Kathleen Spivack, Sylvia Plath, and Anne Sexton. Lowell was a "liquid poet," a poet prone to constant shifts in style and allegiance.

(Hence, three wives?) His Pulitzer Prize–winning *Lord Weary's Castle* (1946) owes a great deal to the New Critics (Allen Tate and John Crowe Ransom were his teachers); *Life Studies* (1959) owes a great deal to the bold, bald, proto-Confessionalism of Allen Ginsberg and the Beats. In his reminiscence of writing *Life Studies,* Lowell said he was influenced by hearing "Howl" while doing a number of readings on the West Coast. He found himself simplifying his own poems, breaking the meter, making impromptu changes at readings. This shaped a steering from his stress on a highly crafted poem to poems that strove to make a "breakthrough back into life."

I hope I haven't drifted too far from *Where Good Ideas Come From*! Johnson mentions the "adjacent possible" as an essential dynamic in the exchange and influence of ideas between or among intimates. Imagine two or three mates afloat in a small craft, a raft maybe. Surrounding the "adjacent possible" is a slightly larger circle of influence, which Johnson calls the "platform innovation pattern." In poetry, we find that the "platform" model is equivalent to the writing workshops happening in our colleges, public libraries, and living rooms—or in places like the Bread Loaf Writers' Conference or the Cave Canem Retreat for African-American poets. Here the participants are not always close friends; they're like acquaintances on a houseboat or ferry.

Finally, surrounding the "adjacent possible" and "platform" spheres is the "liquid network." The various aforementioned crafts navigate distinct aesthetic seas: the Sea of L=A=N=G=U=A=G=E Poets is a liquid network; the Sea of Spoken Word Poets, the Sea of New Formalists. The liquid network is broad enough to hold people who share common interests/beliefs/aesthetics but don't necessarily interact with one another.

Robert Lowell crossed the borders of various poetics and liquid poetic networks—the Confessionals, the Beats, the New Critics. He was a liquid poet adapting and borrowing and, as Bauman says, "ready and willing to change tactics at short notice, to abandon commitments and loyalties without regret and to pursue opportunities according to their current availability." His liquidity made his relationship to poets and poetry renewable and sustainable—but it also engendered a certain ethical uncertainty (as in the poems featuring the letters of his ex-wife, Elizabeth Hardwick).

6.

"I know their style," Etheridge Knight writes in "The Idea of Ancestry." It suggests his chameleon poetics. He was both more casual and more calculating than Lowell as he drifted between the Liquid Poetic

Networks of the Black Arts Poets, the Deep Image Poets, and even the Academic Networks he toured poeting for a living. The present-day university/MFA decreeing system certainly constitutes the largest of our poetry Liquid Networks. Although the Association of Writers and Writing Programs, as they are known, can vary in aesthetics, they share the same systems of evaluation (grades, teaching, critical studies based on the Cartesian model of logical observation and evidence) and systems of confirmation (degrees, publication, tenure).

Knight had no college degree (he dropped out of school at fourteen and discovered poetry during his eight-year stint in the Indiana State Prison), but he moved between the community workshops he often held in urban dive bars, the bucolic workshops of Robert Bly's annual Great Mother Conference, and the standard workshops such as those he taught as poet in residence at the University of Pittsburgh from 1969 to 1970.

In the 1990s, when I was a graduate student at the University of Pittsburgh seeking something beyond the university's workshop platform, I attended a community workshop every third Saturday. The group held no grad student other than myself, though it took place in the university's Black Studies department. The department had been launched in the early '70s by Sonia Sanchez, when she and Etheridge Knight lived in Pittsburgh. The Kuntu Writers' Workshop had once been attended by August Wilson. By the time I showed up, Wilson was gone, but his close friend Rob Penny, a poet and playwright, was there captaining a motley African-American crew that included: an ex-con ex-heroin addict who'd run, in his heyday, with Etheridge Knight; a few quirky, lusty, elderly sisters; a few steel-mill workers; and Dane the Demented Wordsmith, who was an aspiring rapper and my closest friend in those years.

At twenty-two, with almost no resources, I'd moved to Pittsburgh from South Carolina. I knew no one, I had nothing, I knew nothing. I lived on the instant grits left in the place where, for a summer, I house-sat in lieu of rent. I read many of the books that lined the walls; I fed the owner's two cats; I watched her stash of lesbian porn. The women in those films were like businessmen or scholars. Their breasts were floppy but not uninteresting. I watched them while my stomach growled. I shed ten pounds of muscle. I hung out with Dane, playing basketball, smoking weed, flirting with his sister—and every third Saturday I absorbed the poetics of old-school Black Nationalism.

Rob Penny had not changed his name to Rob X or Rob El Ali Shabazz or anything, but in his *kufi*, *dashiki*, and black turtleneck, he was the classic Black Arts poet: someone whose poetics were rooted in community. The poster child or maybe poster father of the Black Arts aesthetic was none other than the late Amiri Baraka. Baraka, formerly known as LeRoi Jones, was a former liquid poet. As Andrew Epstein writes in *Beautiful Enemies* (2006):

> During a crucial eight-year period as the 1950s turned into the 1960s, Baraka came to embody an exciting experiment in collaboration, friendship, and intertextuality across traditional boundaries of race. . . . Few, if any, major African-American writers have ever been as thoroughly enmeshed in a community of white writers, lovers, and friends as Baraka, and few have so dramatically extricated themselves from this kind of interracial dialogue.

Baraka was for a period a liquid modernist, changing places, spouses, names, values, and orientations. He changed from Jones to Baraka, he divorced his Jewish wife and married a sister, he moved from Greenwich Village to Harlem, he had a "mysterious/ambiguous" relationship with Frank O'Hara. And then his fluidity (and with it his poetics) solidified around the poetics of politics, a poetics of solidarity.

I can admire a purposeful, socially oriented poetics like Baraka's. Certainly Gwendolyn Brooks found the energy of the Black Arts Movement compelling enough to change her style of poetics. Such poetics can and have provided shelters/structures where people come together. In her brief essay "The New Black," she wrote of being stirred by the upheaval she witnessed at the Second Black Writers' Conference at Fisk University in 1967. Poet Elizabeth Alexander's essay "Meditations on 'Mecca': Gwendolyn Brooks and the Responsibilities of the Black Poet" articulates this meeting as well as the ways that Brooks's *In the Mecca* (1968) was "a meditation on the role of art and artist during the troubled times filled with philosophical and strategic challenges for black communities." As Alexander says, Brooks's encounter with the young black poets is immediately discernible in *In the Mecca*, which was explicitly *for and about*: "black people in taverns, black people in alleys, black people in gutters, schools, offices, factories, prisons, the consulate; I wish to reach black people in pulpits, black people in mines, on farms, on thrones." It's a clear and curious statement since Brooks's poems always, in fact, engaged black people, though not always as an explicit statement of blackness.

In addition to Brooks's *In the Mecca* and Knight's *Poems from Prison*, 1968 saw the publication of *Black Fire: An Anthology of Afro-American Writing*, co-edited by Larry Neal and Amiri Baraka, which is "often considered a seminal work from the Black Power Movement." Neal and Baraka were also contributors, along with poets like Sonia Sanchez, Victor Hernández Cruz, and Stanley Crouch. Black women poets Audre Lorde, whose debut collection, *First City*, appeared that year, and Lucille Clifton, whose *Good Times* debuted a year later, were *not* included, highlighting the anthology's and the movement's narrowness in terms of "nationhood" (which was closer to *man*hood: there are only four women among the more than forty men). Gwendolyn Brooks and Etheridge Knight, who were both closely associated with the Black Arts Movement (and its editors) by 1968, also were omitted from the anthology.

Be that as it may, I'm placing them at the nexus of the new Black Arts poetry that 1968 birthed. These poets, along with Baraka, influenced the Black Arts Movement just as much as the movement influenced them.

I'm thinking of reciprocal influence of the sort art critic Michael Baxandall describes in *Patterns of Intention: On the Historical Explanation of Pictures* (1985). "'Influence' is a curse of art criticism primarily because of its wrong-headed grammatical prejudice about who is the agent and who the patient," Baxandall says, insisting the river of influence flows in at least two directions: "Arts are positional games and each time an artist is influenced he rewrites his art's history a little."

One could argue that Black Arts poetry had never been represented so broadly. Born within a few years of each other—Amiri Baraka, Sonia Sanchez, and Audre Lorde were born in 1934, Lucille Clifton in 1936—that generation rewrote poetry's history more than "a little." Their work differed from the prescribed "Black Arts poem" because it moved from the abstraction of black manifestos to the intimacy of black lives. If anything, 1968 marks a nexus of new black poetry—a moment of poetry so diverse no particular philosophy could hold it. Brooks and Knight are notable in the midst of the social and aesthetic shifts *because of* their poetic shifts. Their styles are liquid.

Baraka ceased being liquid. Sylvia Plath was liquid, though her evolution from *The Colossus* to *Ariel* is abbreviated by suicide; Adrienne Rich and Audre Lorde were liquid. The idea of liquidness (fluidity? liquidity?) is not limited by race, class, or gender—the more oppressed or disenfranchised one is, the more important is one's liquidness.

74

7

Well, maybe that's not completely true. A few poets outside any manner
of network have also had their influence. Wallace Stevens, for example,
seems contrary to any notion of the shifting, adaptive poet. Appropri-
ately, in Stevens even water is not fluid—or it is only as fluid as snow.
(Snow was once liquid and will be again.) Snow is everywhere in his
poems. As evidence, here is a cento: a poem built from the writings of
other authors in such a way that creates new meanings. I wrote it years
ago using a few of Stevens's wintery lines:

> One must have a mind of winter
> To regard the frost and the boughs
> Of the pine-trees crusted with snow
> The light in the room more like a snowy air
> Reflecting snow
> And roses frail as April snow
> Passions of rain, or moods in falling snow
> The sea is in the falling snow
> And in the edges of the snow
> It was snowing
> And it was going to snow
> The wise man avenges by building his city in snow.

I think of that line, "The wise man avenges by building his city in
snow," as some manner of edict against change. Stevens was not liquid
in terms of his poetic network. (That's unfortunately reflective in the
story of his calling Gwendolyn Brooks a coon: *Who's the coon? Who let
in the coon?* he said.) His sense of liquidity was not protean; it was icy
and self-reflective. Can we consider him liquid in terms of imagination?

Depends on your capacity for forgiveness. In my poem "Snow for Wallace Stevens," I write, "Thus, I have a capacity for love without / forgiveness." That's me trying to be a liquid poet. Again, as Baxandall says, "Each time an artist is influenced he rewrites his art's history a little." I had to rewrite Stevens, hence the cento made of his lines, to love him. But I don't forgive him, and more importantly, he doesn't care. I love this in Stevens, too. That he does not pander to his audience. I suggest he even held a bit of disdain for audiences, the democracy of approval, consensus, accessibility. I suggest he valued the idiosyncratic reader. The individual reader in the company of a single poem has, if I rewrite Stevens correctly, a deeper patience and empathy. It's a more personal, more fluid relationship. That's what Stevens teaches me. Reading Stevens, I trust feeling more than meaning. I realize I do not believe it is the poet's job to mean. Feeling means more than meaning.

I realize I may only want to talk to poetry lovers. No one scolds a basketball player for talking little more than basketball. During postgame interviews, there are platitudes about God and Momma, but the comments return invariably to basketball. It is what the basketball player knows. Basketball fans and players approve. I realize I am only interested in interested parties. I realize I have never loved tap dancing, for example. I do not love the way tap dancers shuffle on their heels and toes, or that while doing so they are often smiling and (even worse) sometimes clapping as if to applaud the onlookers for looking.

8.

I sat drinking Johnnie Walker Blue with Dane after his first child was born. This was maybe ten years after those Saturday community workshops. Rob Penny, Rest in Peace, was dead. Dane's dream of becoming a rapper was dead. At $300 a bottle, Johnnie Walker Blue was nothing I could afford, but I'd heard it was the drink Maya Angelou demanded backstage anytime she was invited to a reading. I'm not sure who mentioned the story. Probably some black tenure-track poet who'd met Dr. Angelou at a university reading and been selected as the one lucky enough to pour Maya (as my kind of black folk called her) a short glass of the mythic, magical elixir. I'd heard it was the equivalent of liquid heroin and knew as soon as I had the money I'd buy myself a bottle. I thought if I drank enough Johnnie Walker Blue, I'd be able to leave my body. Maybe it would result in a poem. Never happened. I've bought two bottles over the years. The last time I drank Johnnie Walker Blue, I was morbidly blue and lonely, emptying the bottle in an empty room. But the first time I bought a bottle was around the time Dane's daughter was born. He was my closest friend in Pittsburgh. Like family. I'd had kind of a thing with his sister. I can remember sucking her fingers once before we made love. This was the night she showed up on my doorstep weeping and terrified. She'd been tied up by some thugs looking for Dane or Dane's stash of drugs. She's a lawyer now, so I shouldn't be telling you about any of that if I don't want to be sued. (Let's call it an excerpt from "A Story Called Poetic Liquids.")

9.

The poem is a kind of house. I have been talking about poetics, that is to say, sensibility and tactic, but when I think of engaging the resulting poem, I think of houses. Some are bungalows, some are cabins, cottages, McMansions, etc. One enters through the front door and is housed in language. Each room is a tangible space possessed of a table, a coatrack, chairs, rugs, and the accoutrements of entertainment and distraction: a stereo, a television, books on a bookshelf. And should we find a couch in the kitchen, order says the couch must be moved to the den. But how wonderful to find use for a couch in the kitchen, a fridge in the bathroom. Order demands we place the objects of our homes in all the expected places. But how wonderful to find your mother reclining on the couch while she stirs a pot of something delicious. If I tell you my father often stared intently into an opened refrigerator as he sat on the toilet, you might call the image surreal and whimsical or maybe gross—though long ago my father was exiled to the lower quarters of the house, my mother's house. The whale snores that issued from his mouth when he slept made the pictures on the wall tremble. I thought the snores would kill him, I thought he might choke on dark air. My mother sentenced him to the room directly below her bedroom along with his pressed corrections-officer uniforms (I suppose she returned hers to the state when she retired), his three or four pairs of black prison-guard shoes yawning relief that his swollen feet were removed, a white sheet, and a dissonant floral quilt. My mother determined the floral fashion of house linen, my mother decided the floral fashion of furniture, my mother decided who slept where. She was our warden, unchallenged, and benevolently indifferent to the closets wherein my father's guns leaned like the friends he made in a twenty-five-year military career. Boxes of stubborn, silent bullets, camouflage, shirts with their medals and glorious patches removed, pants he'd long ago grown too fat to wear. A poem can be understood as a house. A house is a poem.

10.

There is anecdotal evidence of Etheridge Knight's liquidness in his poem "Dark Prophecy: I Sing of Shine," where Shine, the iconic trickster of African-American folklore, is first to escape the sinking *Titanic*. Knight writes:

Yeah, I sing to thee of Shine
and how the millionaire banker stood on the deck
and pulled from his pockets a million dollar check
saying Shine Shine save poor me
and I'll give you all the money a black boy needs—
how Shine looked at the money and then at the sea
and said jump in mothafucka and swim like me—
And Shine swam on—Shine swam on—

This is how one should move in a liquid poetic network. Shine swims between allegiances. When "the banker's daughter ran naked on the deck" promising sex if Shine rescues her, Shine says "you got to swim not fuck to stay alive." His motive is not power or prestige or pussy. His motive is survival. He seeks whatever networks and harbors feed his freedom. His craft is fueled by craftiness and possibility, not ideology or allegiance. I've suggested there are distinct liquid poetic networks, but in truth, it's all the same water. We say there are five oceans on the planet, but in fact, there is only one big ocean divided into Pacific, Atlantic, Indian, Southern, Arctic for the sake of navigation and orientation and, of course, property. Influence does not—or should not—bother with such demarcations. It's really all the same water. Shine aka Knight offers a craft rooted in rootlessness.

II.

Poetics is sometimes considered synonymous with "voice"—and I realize some people will have questions about how I found mine, given my belief in influence and uncertainty. I have two reasons why voice is nothing to pursue:

1. Voice is an intrinsic liquid, born in the blood, so wear all the masks you want.

2. Voice is an enigmatic fluid, too shifty to tie down, so wear all the masks you want.

Listen to Prince sliding between a high-heeled baritone and a mustached falsetto—we always know it's his voice. It's not impossible to imagine it was actually Prince in disguise in *Purple Rain*. It is not impossible to imagine Prince and Morris Day were the same person. Prince was a liquid modern man shifting between names and styles, octaves and hairdos. He was a man shifting into and out of the voices/ selves he made.

And anyway, sounding like yourself is harder than you might imagine. I mean, do I have a *black voice*? Even if I do, it doesn't give me a leg up. Blackness, like whiteness or Yankeeness or Southernness, is a useful starting place, but it is fortunately susceptible to influence and styles of variation. It is *enriched* by influence and styles of variation. The late, '90s-era rapper Craig Mack says in "Get Down": "My style ain't a style that is a style so I can go buck wild."

The poetics of liquid is the poetics of wind. The poetics of liquid is the poetics of escape, the poetics of doors and windows. The poetics of liquid is the poetics of hallucination. It is the poetics of blood. It is the poetics of feeling. It is akin to the poetics of love, it is akin to the poetics of pleasure. The poetics of liquid is the poetics of hunger. The poetics of liquid is the poetics of the self; the poetics of liquid is the poetics of reflection, reflective minds and reflective mirrors: a place to reverse the place, a face to reverse the face.

Poetics, like voice, can hold multiple registers and experiences and interests; poetics, like a voice, is more than a reflection of identity—a word that lacks both the fluidity of sensibility and the intimacy of personality. Poetics is a reflection of a being *being*.

12.

So yes, I like the idea of the poem as house governed by a sort of feng shui (Chinese, "wind-water") poetics. We enter the rooms but don't always consider the influence of spaces around and between the rooms: the basement, where the unkempt Id and intuition live—or the attic, where big ideas and philosophies float. If a house is a poem, I'd describe my poetic tastes as something like a yard with a fence I cannot see. If I leave my porch and walk over a few hills and meadows, cross a few rivers, I suspect I will find my fence: the border at which I will say *what's inside is a poem, what's outside is not.* I want to test that border; I want to straddle it; I want to remake it. "Make," from the Greek word *poiētēs*, meaning "maker, author, poet."

13.

This is how we arrive at Vico's *verum factum*: Maker's Knowledge. Giambattista Vico (1668–1744) was an Italian rhetorician. He offers a terrific counter to the Cartesian notion of being. René Descartes's notion of knowledge prizes deductive reasoning and observation over perception. With Vico it is not "I think therefore I am" but "I make therefore I grasp." According to Vico, we can know only what we make: computers, cars, systems of government; what we have not made we cannot know: the universe, the mind, the soul. Can the self be created? Does art create the self, or does art affirm the self? Vico offers a kind of knowledge that has room for uncertainty. Moreover, this suggests that the way to engage art is to make art; the best way to grasp the wonder of poetry is to make poetry. Making involves action, not deduction. It involves wading into the restless liquid of language.

Vico provides an answer to Steven Johnson's implicit question: *Where [Do] Good Ideas Come From?* From other ideas. And good poems come from other poems. It is not enough to reach after uncertainty in the act of negative capability. One hopes to make something out of that uncertainty. Zygmunt Bauman proposes a fluidity that makes a *practice* of uncertainty (chance, risk) and influence. Liquidity makes one open not only to friendships and networks but also to everything everywhere. One's relationship to words and worlds is always anxiously in flux, but with unpredictability come endless currents of potential, discovery, and inventiveness. Once, on a panel about political poetry, I said I distrusted dogma, edicts, generalities about anyone and anything—and an older co-panelist (a stalwart political poet) told me that everyone has to choose a side. Maybe he was right when it comes to living. But in art —in poetry—choosing sides and styles congeals/hardens/ends the conversation I want to have with the world.

14.

With the publication of my most recent poetry book, I realized that a poem *transparently* influenced by Etheridge Knight has appeared in every other book I've written. In my debut was "Poet Dying at the Window," a poem in conversation with Knight's love poem "As You Leave Me." In my third book was "The Blue Etheridge," the persona poem I

83

share on page 146. Today the ending image of that poem seems pertinent: Knight on a bridge above the waters of change, while his own barrel-backed shadow aims to still those waters, says something about the desire for both movement and resolution. The two paradoxical gestures equal uncertainty. I realize I am not so interested in resolving the conflict between influence and invention as much as I am in acknowledging the blurred space between them. "The only thing stronger than my joy is my hunger for joy. It's a fact, the bones of a horse last longer than the horse." These are lines from "Portrait of Etheridge Knight in the Style of a Crime Report," the Knight poem in my 2015 collection, *How to Be Drawn*. It's not a poem I've ever read aloud—or know how to read aloud—as it takes the shape of an actual crime report. Poems can take the shape not only of other poems but of all other forms: recipes, glossaries, powerpoints, obituaries. Just as metaphor is based on comparisons, links, bridges, so too poetry bridges, synthesizes, transforms. Like water it does not give in so much as give away, give a way. Poetry is where we influence and are influenced by what influences us. Poetry is where we shape and take the shape of what shapes us. I'm calling this *The Poetics of Liquid*.

LINE 18: AN EMPTY SPACE

During the war I was a member of the Corpse Corps. Our job was transporting the dead from the battlefield, to the field morgue, and on to the flag-covered coffins waiting at the airport. Sometimes nothing but body parts were shipped back home.

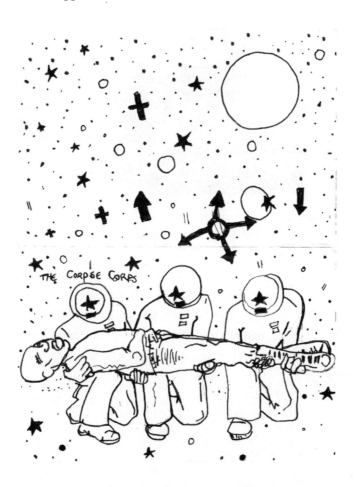

Boys too small for battle fired their rifles above the heads and head-stones in salute. It was an elaborate, elegiac affair for what was some-times no more than bandages and stitches. I know because I was the resident storyteller of the Corpse Corps. Sometimes I wrote letters to the kinfolk of the dead. Everything real I covered in the oil of fiction. My yarns, fables, and folktales slid seductively into truths. I put my brothers in the Corps to sleep with prayers disguised as stories.

Late one night, after stories about bravery and pussy, I told the one or two men not yet asleep a story about my grandmother, whose surname was Watermaker and whose four children had different fathers and different patronyms: Giambattista Washington Jr.; Delores was my mother, Lavish River's middle name; Beulah Jenkins; Ceasar-Ray Seabrooks. A voice not far off in the darkness asked if the four children represented the four points of the weather vane. I said, Hell no, that's crazy. I think the voice belonged to a newbie, a young brother poorly prepared to scavenge the carnage. Stupefied, he had not slept for two or three nights. He was awake, at least for the little while he was alive, for all my stories. He said sometimes I'd continue talking, mumbling the rhythm of a tale well after I'd fallen asleep.

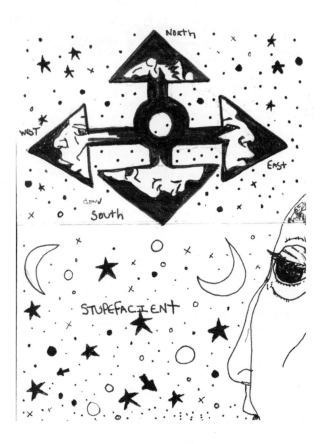

I never knew the name of my grandmother's first husband, an ash-colored man she married at fifteen. He never returned to our village after the war. They had no children. Later all the fathers of her misbegotten babies vanished similarly. Soon after the second child was born with a horn sprouting from his brow, a police car carried his father away. The elder daughter began speaking in some defunct African tongue exactly thirty-one days after she was born. Her father was killed in a New Jersey casino. In New Jersey he had a wife, two cars, and twins. Watermaker was his mistress down south. Brother Insomniac said from the darkness, "Damn, man, you come from a tribe of bastards. No wonder I can't believe half the shit you say."

I told him the four children represented the four horsemen of our apocalypse: our religion, our opulence, our loyalty, our ambition. They were our bastards raised by the Maker of Water alone. The horsemen were riding toward us thoroughly covered in rain, I said half to myself. Before I knew it, I was dreaming again of the war. I was making my way through a field of limbs and torsos with no attachments.

I saw the face of Brother Insomniac in the mud beside me. Though he appeared to be sleeping, he spoke the names of my grandmother's children when I kneeled to grasp him. Giambattista, which means John the Baptist, Lavish, Beulah, Ceasar-Ray.

LINE 21: WHEREABOUTS
UNKNOWN

One Saturday night Mr. K was seen in a corner of the neighborhood bar shaking hands with a deputy of darkness. One afternoon in the public library Mr. K was seen leaning over a geography book. When he slipped out just before the library closed, he left behind a trail of blue salt. Sometimes Mr. K took the shape of a snake doctor selling a concoction of moonshine and sugar as a guaranteed elixir for good health. In Korea he claimed to have slept in the arms of someone called "The Hunger Nurse." In Indiana he was seen covered in camouflage. The mud around his father's grave covered his boots. In prison he disappeared whispering the same word over and over to himself. The whereabouts of half the poems he thought up in solitary confinement remain unknown. Once or twice Mr. K was seen skipping down the steps of a courthouse. The whereabouts of the poems written on bar napkins remain unknown. One Sunday Mr. K shouted from the back of a Memphis preacher's congregation: "I'll hop to heaven on one foot before I ride there on your goddamned bus!" One evening in Pittsburgh Mr. K sold the dogs of his stepchildren for dope. The whereabouts of the poem written during Mr. K's weekend locked in a Connecticut jail remain unknown. Sometimes K stood for Quixotic, Candor, Knuckler, Confessor. During the course of one weekend in Minneapolis Mr. K borrowed money from three poets, one poet's girlfriend, one poet's wife, another poet's ex-wife, and a former poetry student. The whereabouts of the poems written in methadone clinics remain unknown. The whereabouts of the poems written in hospitals and hotel rooms remain unknown. One evening he was spotted smoking with a janitor while people wearing suits and Sunday dresses waited to hear him speak. Once Mr. K is said to have told an audience of high schoolers in Michigan, "The memory of living always lasts longer than actually being alive." The whereabouts of the poem he wrote the night before he threw himself a wake remain unknown. The whereabouts of the poem that ends "The poems change as I am trying to change" remain unknown.

LINE 22: THE GRAVES

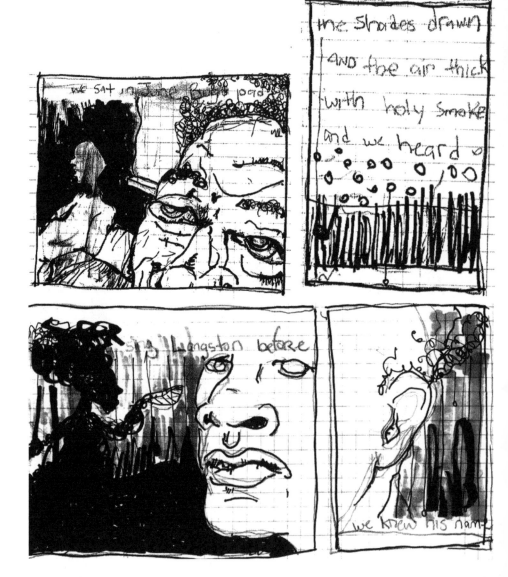

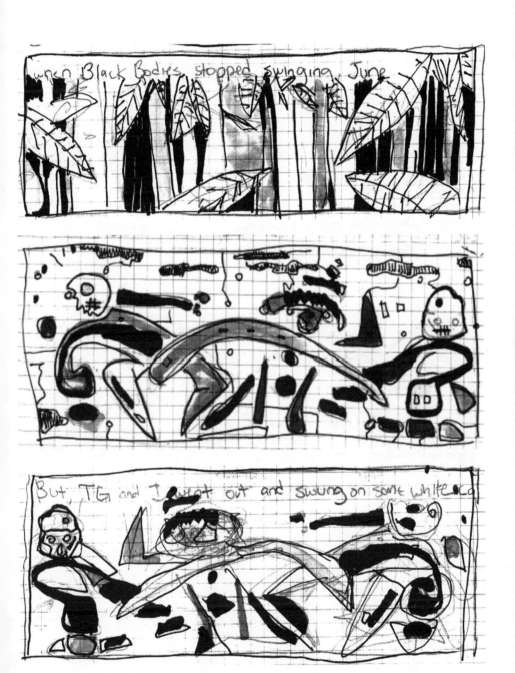

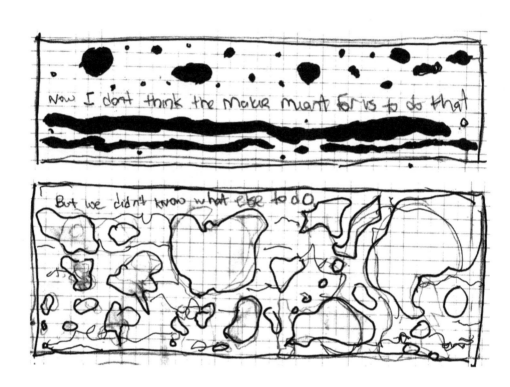

Now I don't think the maker meant for us to do that

But we didn't know what else to do.

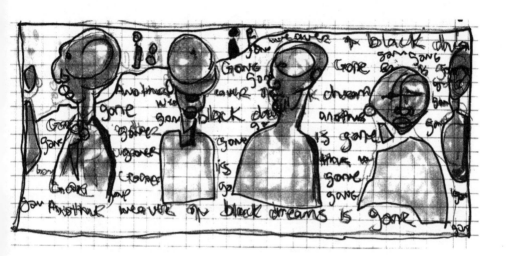

LINE 24: MESSAGES

I. THE MESSAGE OF THE MOUNTAIN STANDING IN THE WAY

Whether you like it or not,
your genes have a political past,
your skin, a political cast,
your eyes, a political slant.

WISŁAWA SZYMBORSKA,

"Children of Our Age"

In 1806, Fisher Ames, the anti-Jeffersonian Federalist, offered a fairly simple definition of politics: "Politicks is the science of good sense, applied to public affairs." He likely was not thinking about the particular politics of race, gender, or class, but these certainly fall under the roof of "public affairs." Race, especially as it relates to black and white Americans, fills a very big room in our very big house of public affairs: economic affairs, cultural affairs, moral affairs. Race provides many a rich and varied and tactile case study in politics and, my chief concern here, in how one might bridge poetry and politics. A political cast, a political past gives each of us an unavoidable political slant. The question is how might that slant be represented? More than theoretical answers, this essay aspires to prompt a few poetic ventures for you,

Reader. I'd like you to write your poems in the spirit of Maker's Knowledge. Know-how comes through creation not deduction. Not "I think therefore I am," but "I make therefore I grasp." For example, you might use the following quote from "The Negro Artist and the Racial Mountain," Langston Hughes's 1926 political/aesthetic manifesto, to write your own political/aesthetic manifesto: "No great poet has ever been afraid of being himself." Hughes, who was twenty-four at the time, was applying "the science of good sense" to black life: "This is the mountain standing in the way of any true Negro art in America," he wrote, "this urge within the race toward whiteness, the desire to pour racial individuality into the mold of American standardization, and to be as little Negro and as much American as possible."

Although Hughes doesn't use the words *politics* or *political*, the essay was written in direct response to a debate about the politics of blackness. *The Nation* had solicited him to write a response to "The Negro-Art Hokum," prominent black journalist George Schuyler's essay arguing against black aesthetics. "Because a few writers with a paucity of themes have seized upon imbecilities of the Negro rustics and clowns and palmed them off as authentic and characteristic Aframerican behavior, the common notion that the black American is so 'different' from his white neighbor has gained wide currency. . . . Why should Negro artists of America vary from the national artistic norm?" Schuyler wrote, insisting what others called *cultural distinctions* were simple Negro stereotypes. Hughes's response appeared a week after Schuyler's essay was published.

The Nation's and George Schuyler's pivotal roles in the essay's origins have faded, but Hughes's insistence that young Negro artists use their art to declare, "I am a Negro—and beautiful," has certainly endured. Decades after the Harlem Renaissance, we could hear Hughes in the "Black Is Beautiful" chants of the sixties and seventies. We can hear it echoed in today's Black Lives Matter chants. Or some of us hear it. Those who retort "All Lives Matter" seem to hear in the assertion, "Black Lives Matter *more than other lives*." I hear it as, "Black Lives Matter *as much as other lives*." It can appear Hughes only matters to blacks. He and the implications of his essay matter as much as other poets and assertions about American poetry. His notion of black poetics—a poetry placing black life at its nexus—is not so different from Confessionalism, a poetry placing a poet's life at its nexus. Certainly, Robert Lowell would have written about his blackness (he comes close in "For the Union Dead") had he been black; certainly Sylvia Plath would have written about her blackness (she almost did with that "nigger eye" in "Ariel") had she been black. To suggest (as some might) the difference is "private" versus "public" underestimates the overlap of private and public life. Hughes makes no distinction between personal and political life in his essay, but nonetheless his message endures as a call for a black solidarity, seemingly ignored by all other writers. I have never read or heard a white poet claim to have been influenced by "The Negro Artist and the Racial Mountain." What would that influence look like? "No great poet has ever been afraid of being himself." What his essay suggests is not so different from Schuyler: art reflecting a particular, personal perspective. The essay is political not simply because it values black life but because it values all cultural and creative self-determination.

Where Hughes's essay was a benchmark statement of the Harlem Renaissance, forty years later Amiri Baraka's poem "Black Art" was a marker for the Black Arts Movement. Baraka first recorded a reading of the poem with a group of jazz musicians (including Albert Ayler on tenor saxophone, Don Cherry on trumpet, and Sonny Murray on drums—the poem appears on Murray's album *Sonny's Time Now*) in 1965, the year of Malcolm X's assassination. When Baraka later recollected the aims of the movement, he said: "We wanted an art that would actually reflect black life and its history and legacy of resistance and struggle!" His poem "Black Art" is, according to his Black Art compatriot Larry Neal, an "amplification of the new aesthetics." It opens immediately with a surreal almost absurd series of assertions about these "new aesthetics": "Poems are bullshit unless they are / teeth or trees or lemons piled / on a step." After some scandalous, brazen, provocative race moments, the poem issues an outrageous and outraged call to action: "We want 'poems that kill.' / Assassin poems, Poems that shoot / guns. Poems that wrestle cops into alleys / and take their weapons. . . . Let there be no love poems written / until love can exist freely and / cleanly."

Hughes's essay ends with a similar albeit less vitriolic call to action:

Let the blare of Negro jazz bands and the bellowing voice of Bessie Smith singing Blues penetrate the closed ears of the colored near-intellectuals until they listen and perhaps understand. . . . We younger Negro artists who create now intend to express our individual dark-skinned selves without fear or shame.

The great irony: forty years later, Langston Hughes found Baraka and the new younger Negro artists influenced by his call for "individual dark-skinned selves [writing] without fear or shame" a little too fearless and shameless.

Fuck poems
and they are useful, wd they shoot
come at you, love what you are,
breathe like wrestlers, or shudder
strangely after pissing.

Baraka intensified Hughes the way John Coltrane's sax intensified
Charlie Parker's sax; the way Jordan's dunks intensified the dunks of
Dr. J. In fact, maybe it's better if you use Baraka's poem as a model for
expressing your own intense political slant. What would that look like,
a counter to Baraka's "Black Art"—a complication, an intensification,
a moral enhancement?

    If you know the Baraka poem, you know I'm trying to get you into
trouble. *But if a political poem has no interest in troubling and trouble, can
we call it a political poem?* I remember a young white brother, the tattoo
peeking over his V-neck Wu-Tang T-shirt said thug-something—"thug
lives" or "thug lives," it might have been "thug loves"; I might have
imagined it—presenting his Baraka imitation, a burlesque tongue-in-
cheek reversal, to workshop. I'm sure it wasn't called "White Art,"
though he mostly simply said the opposite of everything Baraka said.
Though he was a serious Baraka acolyte, you can imagine the look in
the eyes of the two black students, one the daughter of African immigrants, the other a black middle-class Catholic kid—you can imagine
the looks of shock and suspicion in their eyes. Was the white guy a little
too ecstatic? Maybe someone used, not for the first time, the word *ap-
propriation*, but it might have been *appropriate* that was used. Should we
and how might we distinguish politics from provocation? Supreme
Court Justice Potter Stewart's definition of pornography provides the

only useful answer: you know it when you see it. And then you must trust that you *know* what you're *seeing* or accept that you *do not* know and continue *trying* to see it. To navigate the well-meaning white student's poem required not a moment of clarity but a moment of negative capability—of fertile uncertainty.

2. THE MESSAGE OF POWER

Langston Hughes wrote "The Negro Artist and the Racial Mountain" at the tender age of twenty-four when he was still a student at Lincoln University. This is at least as amazing as Keats writing about negative capability at the age of twenty-two. Maybe Keats would have refined his theory, had he aged. Hughes, as the record shows, made some noteworthy political refinements over time. In the 1920s and '30s when in his twenties and thirties, he wrote direct, often sociopolitical (communist-tinged) poetry. By the 1940s, when he was middle-aged, he began to cloak his political ideas in prose. Most notably in his weekly newspaper columns featuring a sort of trickster, maybe Hughesian alter ego called Jesse B. Simple. As Arthur P. Davis wrote in his 1954 article on the character, Hughes gave "Simple all of the modern Negro's militancy and impatience with compromise.... No professional Negro leader, no Harlem orator, no follower of Marcus Garvey is more concerned about the fate and well-being of the black brother than Simple." One example of Hughes's political views filtered through Simple occurs in a 1949 column titled "Simple Declares Be-Bop Music Comes from Bop! Bop! Bop! Mop!" "Every time a cop hits a Negro with his billy club, that old club says BOP! BOP! ... BE-BOP. ... That's why so many white folks don't dig Bop," Simple explains. "White folks do not get their heads beat *just for being white*. But me—a cop is liable to grab me almost any time and beat my head." (What's that old adage, "The more things stay the same, the more things stay the same"?)

While Hughes couched the violence of police in anecdotal humor, Baraka's "Black Art" dreamed of violent retaliation: "[We want] poems that wrestle cops into alleys / and take their weapons leaving them dead / with tongues pulled out." I know that's hard-core even as cartoonish fantasy. A poem rooted in reality or realism would surely be just as challenging. Audre Lorde's "Power," from *Between Our Selves* (1976), for example, depicts police violence with a journalistic, confessional eye/I and is just as hard-core:

> The policeman who shot down a 10-year-old in Queens
> stood over the boy with his cop shoes in childish blood
> and a voice said "Die you little motherfucker" and
> there are tapes to prove that. At his trial
> this policeman said in his own defense
> "I didn't notice the size or nothing else
> only the color." And
> there are tapes to prove that, too.

Audre Lorde said in an interview that the poem was a direct response to the news that a jury on which a black woman sat had acquitted a policeman in the shooting of an unarmed ten-year-old named Clifford Glover: "I was going across town on Eighty-eighth Street and I had to pull over. A kind of fury rose up in me; the sky turned red. I felt so sick. I felt as if I would drive this car into a wall, into the next person I saw. So I pulled over. I took out my journal just to air some of my fury, to get it out of my fingertips. Those expressed feelings are that poem." *If a political poem is not current, can it be an effective political poem?* Lorde's poem certainly feels current. Unarmed black people continue being shot by policemen.

In June 2015, a twenty-one-year-old white man murdered nine black church members in Charleston, South Carolina. Presently, anything I write frays—that's the verb that comes to mind—even my sentence a moment ago had to be stated as simply as possible to hide its fraying impulses. A twenty-one-year-old white man hoping to begin a race war—twenty-one is not the age of a boy, though he looked to be a bony boy waving a Confederate flag—a twenty-one-year-old claiming to be radicalized after the Trayvon Martin "case"—he's just about Martin's age—it was not a "case," really, was it—a twenty-one-year-old white man radicalized by black-on-white violence murdered six black women and three black men during Wednesday night Bible study at the 199-year-old Emanuel African Methodist Episcopal Church of Charleston, South Carolina. My home state.

There is, of course, a chance the writer using current events will be overwhelmed by emotion: despair, frustration, crippling outrage. In "Power," Lorde uses journalism and intimate confession to create visceral, real-time witness. "I have not been able to touch the destruction within me," she writes in the poem's final stanza:

> But unless I learn to use
> the difference between poetry and rhetoric . . .
> one day I will take my teenaged plug
> and connect it to the nearest socket

raping an 85-year-old white woman
who is somebody's mother
and as I beat her senseless and set a torch to her bed
a greek chorus will be singing in 3/4 time
"Poor thing. She never hurt a soul. What beasts they are."

Must a poem engage violence in some way if it is to be a political poem? "Poems are bullshit unless they are / teeth," begins Baraka's "Black Art." The end of Lorde's "Power" does not articulate "the difference between poetry and rhetoric" so much as articulate the violent consequences of not knowing the difference.

3. THE MESSAGE OF THE CHANGE

Fifty years after Hughes wrote, "An artist must be free to choose what he does, certainly, but he must also never be afraid to do what he must choose," Etheridge Knight said:

> Any black artist whose main theme is not enslavement has to be lying or crazy, because the most real thing to a human being is whether he is free or not. And we are not free. Everything else takes second place to that.

Where do white poets figure in this charge? They don't seem especially free when it comes to writing about race. There's Sharon Olds's "On the Subway" from her 1987 collection, *The Gold Cell,* and more recently, Martha Collins's *Blue Front* (2006), a book-length poem based on a lynching her father witnessed when he was five years old, and *White Papers* (2012), a series of poems questioning what it means to be "white" in a multiracial society. A line from Olds's "On the Subway" underscores the nature of the work in those brave important books: "He is black / and I am white, and without meaning or / trying to I must profit from his darkness." They are repentant; they are steeped in penitence. Tony Hoagland's poem "The Change," on the other hand, is a rarity among rarities as it attempts (successfully or not) to explore/ transgress the dynamics of race *without* expressing explicit guilt or shame. In the poem we find a white voice announcing his own assumptions about blackness and then working through the burden of those assumptions. It opens with a speaker witnessing a tennis match:

> some tough little European blonde
> pitted against that big black girl from Alabama,
> cornrowed hair and Zulu bangles on her arms,
> some outrageous name like Vondella Aphrodite—

A few lines later the speaker stutters toward the confession that makes the poem so troubling or provocative, so political or apolitical, so racist or risky: "I wanted the white girl to come out on top." To the speaker's shock the black tennis player wins. Let's say she wins violently: not only does she defeat Hoagland's "tough little European blonde," she does so without mercy, "[kicking] her ass good" and relishing in that ass kicking. The "unintimidated" black girl displays none of the good sportsmanship, none of the Christian civility MLK promised whites would find awaiting them on the mountaintop, if they repented. I think there are two points of view being expressed in the poem: the speaker who laments the historical change that leads to the defeat and the poet who aspires to the change, but that has been the subject of many a debate among poets. My suggestion for folks troubled by the poem relates to something Saul Bellow once wrote in a letter to a friend, in response to Vladimir Nabokov's *Lolita*, "Suppose we admit it's not too horrible for middle-aged men to copulate with small girls, do we then have to make a philosophy of it?" A brother poet once asked me a similar thing about Hoagland's poem: Just because we know white people have racist feelings, do we need to read their racist poems? My answer is Yes on both counts. If those feelings are shaped into art: Yes.

Bellow went on to say something I like to propose to folks put off by political poems: "I could write a better book from Lolita's point of view." (Oh, if only Bellow had written that book!) Write a better poem from Vondella Aphrodite's point of view. Write a poem, write a novel in the voice of Mark Twain's Jim. Or in the voice of one of Charles Bukowski's girlfriends. One example of how such a POV shift might unfold is Toi Derricotte's "On the Turning Up of Unidentified Black Female Corpses," from *Captivity* (1989). The poem reverses the angle of Henry Taylor's "Landscape with Tractor" from his Pulitzer Prize–winning *The Flying Change* (1985). Where Taylor's quatrains use second-person address as the protagonist discovers the corpse of a black woman while mowing a lawn, Derricotte's quatrains use a first-person point of view that identifies with the corpse. The poem is a reversal without simply indicting the white poet's perspective. (*Is it enough to simply witness/expose the crime? If a political poem points no finger, is it not a political poem?*)

The late Wanda Coleman specialized in sardonic reversals. In *Mercurochrome* (2001), she imitates, translates, subverts, and upends the styles of dozens of canonical poets. There's "Dream Song 811," after John Berryman; "Supermarket Surfer," after Allen Ginsberg. Coleman's "To the Head Nigger Wench in Charge" begins, "I wanted to be sure I left my mark on you," after Frank O'Hara's "To the Harbormaster," which begins, "I wanted to be sure to reach you." The final tercet of Elizabeth Bishop's "Little Exercise":

> Think of someone sleeping in the bottom of a row-boat
> tied to a mangrove root or the pile of a bridge;
> think of him as uninjured, barely disturbed.

becomes, in Coleman's "Consciousness Raising Exercise":

> Think of hundreds sleeping in history's tar
> As still as redwood or mounds of shoes; think
> Of them deeply injured, as disturbances unresolved.

A poem responding to a poem may seem fairly rudimentary, but it is at the root of how we understand art—and by extension, understand others and ourselves. It is an act of Maker's Knowledge. I think, not incidentally, of the Serena Williams section in Claudia Rankine's *Citizen* as a POV reversal of Hoagland's poem. (Some of you may recall her discussion of the poem at the 2011 AWP.) A question Rankine explores in *Citizen*, "What does a victorious or defeated black woman's body in a historically white space look like?" is the same question Hoagland seems to explore in "The Change."

4. THE MESSAGE OF "FOR LANGSTON HUGHES"

After the grand jury declined to indict Officer Darren Wilson in the shooting death of Michael Brown, a group of Cave Canem poets organized *Black Poets Speak Out* as a response. It was an artistic extension of Black Lives Matter, not unlike the way Black Arts were an extension of the Black Power/Black Panther movement. Hundreds of black poets across the US read the following words before they shared poems: "I am a black poet who will not remain silent while this nation murders black people. I have a right to be angry." I chose Etheridge Knight's "For Langston Hughes." It expresses the heartbreak that can precede anger. In Baraka's "Black Art," the fantasy of violence is animated by a theatrical hysteria. In Lorde's "Power," the anger is animated by powerlessness. "For Langston Hughes" seems, at first glance, to show the grief that can animate violence.

FOR LANGSTON HUGHES

Gone   Gone
  Another weaver of black dreams has gone
we sat in June Bug's pad with the shades drawn
and the air thick with holy smoke. and we heard
the Lady sing Langston before we knew his name.
and when Black Bodies stopped swinging June
Bug, TG and I went out and swung on some white cats.
now I don't think the Mythmaker meant for us to do *that*
but we didn't know what else to do.

Gone   Gone
  Another weaver of black dreams has gone

What strikes me about the poem is not just the depiction of grief, but the confusion between the grief and violence. "We didn't know what else to do," he writes. It reminds me of the violence in Ferguson and

Baltimore. Media coverage is always heavy on disdain when riots occur. Martin Luther King, Rodney King: rioting feels like a default response at this point. At such moments rioting is a strategy; an act hovering somewhere between anarchy and revolution. The only other option is to do nothing. Violence becomes a form of political action. Destruction, even when it's self-destruction, becomes a viable response to a failed state. Fortunately, art gives us a means to make our angers, our frustrations, our fantasies, and of special interest to me, our confusions tangible. The poems by Baraka, Lorde, and Hoagland express the confusion during and before and sometimes after political action. The confusion is often tied to vulnerability. Confusion over a shifting social dynamic in "The Change," confusion over the justice system and the black woman who participates in exonerating the white policeman after he guns down the ten-year-old black boy in "Power." Confusion bleeds and belts into slapstick and/or delirium in "Black Art."

But while the confusions in these poems are directed and managed, the various confusions in and around Knight's poem could prompt one to ask whether it is a political poem at all. The moment he tells us about the "holy smoke" we could rightly say, these dudes aren't grieving revolutionaries, they're just high. What moves the poem into the sphere of political poetics involves its blend of confusion and fantasy. For one thing, Knight was actually still in jail when Hughes died from complications related to prostate cancer. Thus, the reaction to his death and, by extension, the reaction to the song "Strange Fruit" are imagined actions. Furthermore, even if this was actually based on something Knight and his friends actually did after hearing "Strange Fruit," the whole poem remains a fantasy in ways not even the author seems to recognize. Because contrary to what Knight says in his introduction to the poem, Langston Hughes did *not* write "Strange Fruit." Call it an example of literal *political incorrectness*.

"Strange Fruit," as we of the information age know, was written by Abel Meeropol, a Jewish high school teacher in the Bronx, after seeing a lynching photograph. (Meeropol, who'd later be investigated for communist sympathies, adopted the orphaned sons of Julius and Ethel Rosenberg.) He published the poem in a teacher's union publication and a Marxist journal and later shared a song version with a club owner who subsequently gave it to Billie Holiday. John Hammond, who had discovered Holiday as a teenager and produced her records at Columbia, called the song "artistically the worst thing that ever happened to her." Holiday, he lamented, had become "the darling of left-wing intellectuals" and homosexuals because of it. *Time* magazine denounced "Strange Fruit" in 1939 as "musical propaganda" for the NAACP. (Ironically, the same magazine named it the song of the century in 1999.) That's all to say the song was politically charged from the very beginning. Could/would Langston Hughes have written such a controversial song?

In 1940, the same year "Strange Fruit" climbed to #16 on the *Billboard* charts, Hughes wrote a friend to say he was "laying off political poetry for a while" and going back "to nature, Negroes, and love." He hoped his new work would replace the more controversial poetry of his youth. That didn't quite happen. In 1953, Joseph McCarthy and the House Un-American Activities Committee (HUAC) asked him to definitively "repudiate [his] former writings and philosophy." "It is always quite refreshing and comforting to know that any Communist or Communist sympathizer has discovered the error of his ways," one of the committee members said to Hughes, "and I was hoping that you would have some real evidence of your change, that you have done and are doing what you can to make amends for whatever damage you may have done by previous writing." Hughes capitulated. "In some countries people are governed by rulers, and ordinary folks can't do a thing about it," he said. "But here all of us are a part of democracy. By taking an interest in our Government, and by treating our neighbors as we would like to be treated, each one of us can help make our country the most wonderful country in the world."

Such statements no doubt have contributed to the enduring image of a gentle and genteel Hughes. He lives in the canon as a poet who seems more social than political. In fact, biographer Arnold Rampersad opened the second volume of his Hughes biography with a quote Hughes wrote to himself a decade after the trial: "Politics can be the graveyard of the poet." It seems far from mountaintop aspirations of a twenty-four-year-old Hughes, but it's only a partial excerpt of Hughes's note. A few lines later he writes: "Concerning politics, nothing I have said is true. A poet is a human being. Each human being must live within his time, with and for his people, and within the boundaries of his country. Therefore, how can a poet keep out of politics? Hang yourself, poet, in your own words. Otherwise you are dead."

As the sixty-something Hughes meditates on the role of politics and poetry, we see how one truth—the poet exists within the boundaries of his country and people—complicates but does not cancel out the twenty-something Hughes's self-determinism: "We build our temples for tomorrow, strong as we know how, and we stand on top of the mountain, free within ourselves." One venturing in the space between art for others and art for the self must be simultaneous, contradictory, vulnerable: slanted. Such qualities are evident in the title of Hughes's final book, *The Panther and the Lash: Poems of Our Times* (1967), published shortly after his death. The Panther alludes to "Black Panther," a poem critiquing the strategies of the black-power militancy: "The Panther in his desperate boldness / Wears no disguise, / Motivated by the truest / Of the oldest / Lies." The lash, on the other hand, alludes to what Hughes calls the "white backlash" in his poem "The Backlash Blues."

> You raise my taxes, freeze my wages,
> Send my son to Vietnam.
>
> You give me second-class houses,
> Give me second-class schools.
>
> . . . .
>
> You must think us colored folks
> Are second-class fools.

Like Meeropol's "Strange Fruit," "The Backlash Blues" is now less well known than the protest song Hughes's close friend Nina Simone made of it the year of his death. Perhaps this is the Hughes poem Knight confused with "Strange Fruit." One reviewer of *The Panther and the Lash* criticized Hughes for failing to "take a side politically" in the book: "We are tempted to ask, what are Hughes's politics? And if he has none, why not? The age demands intellectual commitment from its spokesmen." It's hard to read or hear "The Backlash Blues" and still question Hughes's "intellectual commitment" to politics. He was unwavering in his commitment to black culture, but that did not make him immune to political doubt (isn't "doubt" often a byproduct of "intellectual commitment"?). Hughes enacts Fisher Ames's extended definition of politics. Yes, "Politicks is the science of good sense, applied to public affairs, [but], as those are forever changing, what is wisdom to-day would be folly and perhaps, ruin to-morrow.... [Politicks] cannot have fixed principles, from which a wise man would never swerve."

It is in Hughes's swerves and "slants" that a particular, peculiar, unpredictable political aesthetic emerges. The Langston Hughes who might have written "Strange Fruit" was always right there wrestling the Langston Hughes who could not have written it. "For Langston Hughes," unwittingly or not, pays homage to that human mix of conviction and confusion, belief and bewilderment, violence and vulnerability. We come back to a strange politics of negative capability. Maybe there is no true model for a poem. Not long ago I heard a novelist tell a room of her students to use "I am two minds" in a piece of writing. Without further discussion or direction, she left them to it for the next hour. I was in the corridor when the novelist reappeared near the end of the hour, a stack of papers in her hands. I wanted to know her expectations, her aims with the assignment. There were none, she shrugged. "I just realized I needed to make a bunch of copies, so I gave them some busy work." Right. Okay. But inadvertently or not, she'd tapped into what I'm trying to argue for here: a political work with some manner of tension and uncertainty. You need no prompt. You can do it yourself if you commit to at least two minds in the work. Go on that sketchy little tightrope between art for others and art for yourself. What does your political struggle look like? Give it some thought, then give it some shape. Be honest, be stupid, be brave.

LINE 29: I SIPPED
CORNWHISKEY FROM
FRUIT JARS WITH THE MEN

Then all three sat in armchairs at different ends
of the drawing room and were silent.
ANTON CHEKHOV, "Gooseberries"

It was Radi's idea to visit Yusef Komunyakaa in Trenton, New Jersey, one August. He said we should check in on him. Radi and I met in DC, where he'd been working on a literary project—maybe his dissertation —concerned with *visual culture*. It's the only term I can recall from his research, perhaps because our trip felt vaguely like part of his work. We stopped in Maryland along the way to see the paintings of Kerry James Marshall at the Baltimore Museum of Art. We talked as always about art, literature, women, but not so much about what we expected to find in Yusef's company. We did not discuss Reetika and the tragedy of a few years before. Perhaps I was worried I'd be the intruder among them. Radi befriended Yusef at Indiana University before Yusef left for Princeton. He'd also edited Yusef's *Blue Notes: Essays, Interviews, and Commentaries*.

I, on the other hand, had mostly spent time with Yusef at poetry workshops and conferences. Our closest contact had come in Province-town, where I was a student in his workshop. There, too, our interactions mostly included the company of other students. One of those students was Joel Dias-Porter, aka DJ Renegade. Renegade, like Radi, has been a partner in literary crimes and misdemeanors for more than two decades. Come to think of it: I met them both right around the same time. But where I'd met Radi among academics, I'd met Renegade at a writers' conference in Pittsburgh. Whereas Radi was raised, as I was, in South Carolina, Renegade was raised in my adopted home of Pittsburgh. Somehow this seems relevant to the contrasts in their personalities. Renegade was living in DC at the time, but had come to Pittsburgh for the conference. His mother was in the audience. It's the only time I have ever seen him wear a color other than black. (I think he wore an ornately colored sweater, but I could be making that up.) He was reading his Miles Davis poem, "Subterranean Night-Colored Magi."

A few months before meeting Renegade, I was introduced to this wild-haired, oddly named guy who was considering the graduate program at the University of Pittsburgh, where I was a graduate student. The PhD student who'd persuaded Radi to visit Pitt had persuaded me to meet him. Radi and I were peas in a pod, she said. Moments after she introduced us, we were volleying the names of music, movies, and poets. It couldn't have been more than a few hours of jive at a graduate student party. He chose Indiana University over Pitt—the money was better—and I didn't think of him again until I heard Yusef say his name during the workshop in Provincetown two years later. Yusef smiled, I smiled. One us said the name: Radiclani Clytus. Yona Harvey was also in the workshop and sharing a small hotel room with Ta-Nehisi Coates. All of us—Renegade, Yona, Ta-Nehisi, and I—had come to Provincetown hoping to learn from the great poet. I had also come, to be honest, hoping to spend a bit more time with Yona, whom I'd met two months earlier at a poetry retreat for black poets, Cave Canem. Toi Derricotte, my teacher at Pitt, was one of the co-founders. I wasn't jealous that Yona and Ta-Nehisi roomed together. I wasn't thinking Yona and I would ever date, much less marry.

Had I not met Renegade at that conference in Pittsburgh and told him Toi was taking applications for Cave Canem, he would not have traveled back to DC to tell all the young poets he mentored to apply. Yona, being a ride-or-die, poetry-trooping, Howard University senior, was one of the few among them to actually apply. Provincetown was our second meeting. We wrote letters and talked on the phone until meeting again that February at a Black Writers Conference in Philadelphia. The fourth time we met, that April at the AWP in Washington, DC, I proposed. We attended the second Cave Canem that June and married that July.

All the while, little did I know, Radi was in a similar sort of whirlwind romance. I'd lost track of him again as Yona and I moved to Japan for a year, then to Ohio. Then, as if following a ghost I didn't know I was following, when I moved to New Orleans for a job at Xavier University, I discovered Radi had taught there the year before. He'd gotten married to a brilliant fellow masters student at Indiana and taught for a year at Xavier before the two of them were accepted to the doctoral program at Yale. Someone had just sort of mentioned his name in the midst of a story about the dangers of New Orleans. Remember when Radi was robbed in his front yard? Remember when Radi drove that dude with a fresh machete gash in his gut to the hospital? Radiclani Clytus? He left a trail of stories like furniture too big to take with him when he moved. As I would learn over the years of our friendship, Radi was a magnet for adventure. Adventure is a close cousin to crisis; it is also a close cousin to drama. Radi was a magnet for both. I got his information from colleagues in the English department and contacted him at Yale.

When I was invited to participate in the Langston Hughes centennial celebration a little later, I was more excited to hang with Radi than I was to meet Amiri Baraka and Arnold Rampersad. There was a panel during which there may have been talk of Hughes's possible homosexuality and talk of how white and light-skinned critics (see Arnold Rampersad) had diluted Hughes. Rampersad sat rolling his eyes slightly and sighing under his breath when Baraka spoke. Baraka reciprocated with slightly more visible disagreement when Rampersad spoke. Among the emerging poets were Kevin Young, Shara McCallum, A. Van Jordan—all of us invited by Elizabeth Alexander, who taught at Yale at the time. Elizabeth is a significant part of this story, though she doesn't appear in it. She is like a modern-day Gwendolyn Brooks—a poetry advocate and bridge builder. She and I have become close friends over the years. She became good friends with Radi when he was at Yale. There was a party for the young poets. I suppose Radi and his wife, Louise, had housing somewhere in New Haven, but we hung out so late, he and Lou crashed on my hotel floor.

A summer or two later, we took a road trip to South Carolina: Radi, Louise, Yona, our daughter, Ua, and I—Ua must have been two or three then. Yusef and Reetika's son, Jehan, would have been born around that time. I remember walking with Yusef and a pregnant Reetika at a writers' conference. She'd said I should talk to Yusef about being a father. That *I* should give him some advice about being a father, since I had a new baby. Yusef is older than my father, I laughed. Yusef has a daughter that's nearly my age, I said. I didn't think it was a sign of her desperation, anxiety, fear.

When Yusef taught in Indiana, he'd known Etheridge Knight. This drawing is based on a photograph that appears in "Tough Eloquence," an article he published about Knight in 1993. In it he writes:

> In early 1990, a young poet friend, Kenneth May, introduced me to the man who had been leading The People's Workshop at a bar called the Slippery Noodle in Indianapolis. It seemed as though I had known Etheridge for many years. He was kinfolk. There was something in his eyes that reminded me of the men in my family.

I've tried to imagine Yusef in Etheridge's company. What sort of conversation might the young black poet and army vet from Louisiana have with the old black poet and army veteran from Mississippi? Yusef is quiet. In the photo, he casts a side-eyed look at the camera. Etheridge looks like an old farmer or maybe one of the old vets down at that VFW bar Yusef took Radi and me to, that day in Trenton. Yusef was quiet; dudes knew him wherever we went. He'd made friends of carpenters, musicians, veterans—men like I imagine Etheridge Knight to have been, with opinions about art, politics, and music. He'd left friends and ghosts in Indiana when he joined the faculty at Princeton. He'd bought a big Victorian house in Trenton. I thought vaguely of Faulkner when we turned into the driveway. The tall grass, the chipped paint around the door behind which no one seemed to be waiting. Maybe Radi had to call up and tell him we were outside, because suddenly there he was, welcoming us in as if we were his sons coming home—though maybe that's what I wished in my happiness. He was smaller—on a diet, he said. I was thinking about all that had been taken out of him. The house was full of color: paintings, music, a dining room between shades of a mouthwatering orange, a painter's drop cloth half rolled in the corner. And I think even before we took our bags upstairs we must have gone to the kitchen to uncork a bottle of red wine. "Let's let it breathe," Yusef told us, his rambling houseguests, in that accent I can never place. Part Louisiana, part Australia. Maybe a hint of the Midwest. I thought the house, with its clean banisters and wide rooms, was too big for a poet— simultaneously thinking its paintings and furniture were testament to what a life devoted to poetry could yield. I tried to imagine the woman and child who'd been there and were now somehow nowhere. Two or three years earlier, Reetika Vazirani killed Jehan and then herself.

I think I thought it was the price of his talent. That like some poet Robert Johnson he'd made a deal with the devil to become a great poet. He'd neglected too much to become a great poet. It was a stupid thought. It was a way of avoiding a serious confrontation with Reetika's mental illness—and with Yusef; it was what I thought to keep from thinking about it. Yusef showed us around. He showed us our rooms. He said he still had Reetika's unpublished manuscripts somewhere. Either her family didn't want them or hadn't asked for them. Maybe they'd refused to speak to him or he to them. I don't remember. Later he took us to the basement for a game on the pool table he'd purchased the preceding week. Radi began chalking a cue and talking shit while Yusef poured the wine. Radi was easily the most gregarious of the three of us. Whether he made or missed a shot, he said something smart-ass. I laughed; Yusef mumble-hummed the way he does at anything that pleases him: a beautiful woman, a chord progression, a poem. In his workshops, it was a sound meant to praise a student even when the student's poem could not be praised. I'd heard it once or twice—never over more than a line or two, an image—in the Provincetown summer workshop. He didn't speak much. His hum was just about all the validation we needed—or would get. The hum was why we were there.

While Radi and I have always gathered with smoke and drink to talk art, Renegade and I often gather with no drink or smoke (he does not drink or smoke) to debate poems and poets. We agreed Yusef was a great poet but not on why. Renegade believed it mostly had to do with craft: the frequencies of diction and meter, the concrete blocks of imagery, the equations of metaphor. I believed it involved something more intangible than craft, something that could not be measured or taught. In Yusef's case, I believed—still believe—it had something to do with death, the rhythm of death in poems like "Facing It." I bought my first poetry book, *The Best American Poetry 1990*, because it included "Facing It." Judson Mitcham, a poet visiting my college when I was a junior, had first told me about Yusef Komunyakaa. A name so strange Mitcham had to write it down for me. When I saw Yusef's name in the anthology, I bought the book instantly. I didn't understand the poem. I had no one to talk to about it. But I knew it had a lot to do with death.

Yusef met with everyone for a one-on-one poetry conference. Maybe he and Renegade sparred about craft. I think they did. When my conference came, Yusef took me to the house of painter Pat de Groot, widow of the abstract expressionist Nanno de Groot. On several occasions, Yusef has impacted the trajectory of my life in poetry. While Toi Derricotte has always had a direct nurturing influence on my poems, my life, and my career path, Yusef's influence has been similar to his personality: almost casual or maybe flushed with a shyness that could appear casual. In Provincetown, for example, he'd mentioned, in passing, the poet Lynda Hull. She'd died in the region a few years earlier. She'd been his student in Indiana and spouse to his friend David Wojahn. Reading Hull's *Star Ledger*, I found a kindred spirit: a poet who married romanticism and lyricism, song and story. She remains a chief teacher for me. On another occasion Yusef asked whether I'd listened to the musician James Carroll Booker III. I hadn't. When I did hear Booker for the first time, I was so stunned I wrote a suite of poems; I bought a piano and began teaching myself to play it. I told God, myself, and the devil at the crossroads if I ever learned to play as well as Booker, I'd give up poetry. I've been playing now nearly two decades. It'll take another century of daily practice to be half as good as Booker.

This is perhaps what is called "distant influence." Or "chance influence." The influence of an overheard conversation, a wrong turn. This is perhaps the influence of wise company. That night at Pat de Groot's house we listened to jazz below a poster of Elvin Jones, who had been her lover, according to Yusef. She was a lean, angular personality, a surfer Georgia O'Keeffe. A row of her small, minimalist paintings of the local landscape and seascape hung on the walls. When I tried to imagine her with Elvin Jones, Etheridge Knight's face merged with the drummer's dark, muscular face. Yusef and I talked about Etheridge's mysterious past. He said Knight's enlistment papers had been lost. He raised an eyebrow and said he wasn't sure Etheridge had actually fought in the Korean War. His questions often arrived that way: disguised as asides. He nodded his head. We drank whiskey. He dozed off humming while Pat and I waited, looking at nothing in particular. He didn't stir until the music ended.

I was thinking of that night in Provincetown when Radi suggested we visit Yusef in New Jersey. We left his big beauty-filled house and wine-filled bottles twice: both times to meet his friend Larry Hilton. The four of us (Yusef, Larry, Radi, and me) began the night at the jazz club, where Larry managed a band, and ended it in Trenton's only Veterans of Foreign Wars bar. Where Yusef was stylish, handsome in whatever he was wearing, Larry was heavy, disheveled, aloof. His somberness gave him an air of cool. It was clear he was someone Yusef admired. We ordered drinks as a humdrum jazz band warmed up. I can't speak for Radi, but I felt very grown-up and out of place; I was deliriously thrilled to be hanging out with Yusef. When Yusef asked Larry whether he could bring Radi and me by to see his art, Larry ran a suspicious half-open gaze over the two of us, then agreed to a visit the next day. Yusef shot me a look that said: "Get ready for this."

In the years since, Radi, Yusef, and I have talked more about Larry's art treasure than we have about the ghosts shadowing that trip. Artwork hung even in the narrow vestibule between the padlocked door and hall of Larry's place. Inside, the walls were held down by African masks, jazz photographs, and myriad paintings by famous black artists. His woolly cat watched like Anubis from the base of a Richard Hunt sculpture. *Cramped* really doesn't say enough about the artwork-dominated room. *Hemmed in* is not quite right, either. The place was crowded the way a grandmother's house is crowded, artwork replacing the clutter of family history: a grandmother's house filled with portraits of family in outdated hair styles, bowls full of hard candy, lamps with no lightbulbs, candlesticks, clocks, medals, diplomas—a grandmother sitting at a table in the middle of it all beginning nearly every sentence with "Used to be . . ." and "I remember when . . ." Though there were no pictures of family, this was the spirit of Larry Hilton's place: full and empty at the same time.

Larry talked about his collection in a nonchalant monotone that implied he'd given this tour before, maybe to Yusef's other friends, maybe to the collectors and artists of Trenton and far, far beyond. His heavy-lidded eyes skimmed each piece the way a father might skim a room of his children, unwilling to show one child more attention than another. (It is possible that anything that hangs on a wall long enough will become no more than part of the wall? Can you forget how to see beauty if you see it too often?) One of us might have asked him how a man could come to have so much art, or he might simply have told us the story anticipating the question. How it was connected to the circles of jazz musicians he ran with; how he'd began gathering small, almost insubstantial pieces and had through good luck and friendship come to have all he had now: Romare Bearden, Hale Woodruff, Charles Alston,

Gordon Parks, Roy DeCarava. There might have been a Robert Colescott at the top of the stairs. A Jacob Lawrence in a second-floor bedroom. A wood-and-rubber David Hammons contraption might have been propped in the kitchen. Yusef was preoccupied with one of the African masks in the living room.

"How much would you sell this mask for?" he asked Larry. "It might not be for sell," Larry said without even looking at the piece. Among the photos of jazz legends was Jimmy Scott in a suit that seemed, as all his suits did, too big for his small frame. On a photo of Abbey Lincoln, her cigarette tilted at the angle of diva-dom, something was written to Larry in a sprawling scrawl. "You know Abbey Lincoln?" Radi asked. Larry nodded before leading us to the next room, bored as a museum guard. He said he had bigger and more expensive pieces in storage. "I gave up everything for this," he said with shades of regret and pride.

In Chekhov's "Gooseberries," two dudes stroll the countryside before settling at the home of a friend, where the men sit around telling stories to one another. That day with Yusef was a "Gooseberries" experience. We shared music and drink and debates about art. Etheridge was there in spirit. At one point, the protagonist Ivan Ivanych tells the story of his brother who dreamed and schemed until he owned an estate with, for some reason, gooseberry bushes. During a visit, the brother, who has lived a miserly life to acquire the land, serves a plate of gooseberries. Later, "I could hear him, unable to sleep, going again and again to the plate of gooseberries," Ivan Ivanych says. If we had gone into Larry's place and stolen his collection—as we joked we would—where could we have taken it? His house had easily half a million dollars worth of art, but who beyond other men who'd given up everything for art could find any value in it?

Sometimes when I've asked people for stories about Etheridge Knight, I will hear only that he was a junkie. Even the stories of his commitment to poetry feature him asking to borrow money. Yusef's stories about Etheridge were full of gaps and silences. Yusef, himself, was several stories of gaps and silences. His essay on Knight covers the common biographical ground: prison, the war, the blues. He ends elegiacally,

> Tough and eloquent, he was nothing if not a fall guy for beauty and truth, because he believed that the poet was duty-bound to take chances. He was a man who had been roughed up by life, by bad luck, and he had the emotional and physical scars to prove it.

Maybe Etheridge Knight was a Chekhovian sort of storyteller. Perhaps he told Yusef Chekhovian allegories full of elaborate biographical details about those scars. In any case, Yusef is not the sort of person to repeat any of it.

LINE 30: I FLIRTED
WITH THE WOMEN

One day Mary Karr sort of appeared along my path like a brushfire. She's incendiary, combustible, she's a walking flame. She'll light up the whole house or she'll burn that motherfucker down. Recently, when I told her I described her that way to people, she paused and said, "I don't know if that's a compliment or a complaint." I meant it the way she heard it. She is a passionate Texas woman—a bullshitter, a busybody, and a shrewd businesswoman. She is around the age of my mother. She shares my mother's angular intensity and self-consciousness. I met her when I gave a reading at her university one February years ago. Later, as we walked with her students to dinner, she told me what she thought of my performance. Some of my "experiments" made her shake her head. I'd read "Hide," a two-column poem that could be read three different ways. "The poems are not for you, they're for your readers," she said. "Forget that navel-gazing, ain't-I-clever shit people like John Ashbery write," she said, her high heel boots wounding the sidewalk. Her graduate students nodded in agreement. When I said, "I like some of Ashbery's stuff," she snapped: "Quote some lines of your favorite poem!" I couldn't. Earlier in the day when I'd begun gushing over the great, strange "Dream Song 14" by the great, strange John

Berryman, she launched instantly and easily into a recitation of the poem: "Life, friends, is boring. We must not say so," and so on. She recited the poem with the zeal of someone determined to incinerate boredom. Later she would tell me stories of her ex-fiancé, a writer in the department: she was on her back as he straddled and tried to strangle her on the side of the highway. Some totally nuts shit. But that's not what this is about. Before we entered the restaurant, I decided to ask what I believed would clarify our differences of opinion about poetry. "Do you think language is mostly like an animal or a machine?" I asked her. "It's a machine," she said without even having to think about it. "A thing finely wrought in language." We were walking to a Chinese restaurant in downtown Syracuse that night. Cranes leaned beside the buildings under construction and buildings soon to be demolished. Did she believe there was such a thing as a perfect poem? She said, "Definitely." Her graduate students nodded in agreement. "Yes, my father had a sixth grade education. I write poems he can read. I write them slowly, labor over them, because hell, if you're not playing with the big dogs, the ones who have written the perfect works, why play at all?" I happen to believe language is a beast. Language is a little bit Sphinx, a woman's head on a winged lion's body, and a little bit Chimera, a fire-breathing lion's head on a goat body with a serpent's tail. Dragons were embroidered on the black velvet curtains of the restaurant. All through dinner I tried to make my case. "In the beginning was the Word," we are told in the Gospel of John. We are also told the word was made flesh, not that the word was made machine. No one owns language. No one owns the word *blue*. No word can be coaxed or hammered into perfect meaning. Mary tolerated me. The automobile, the pacemaker, those are fine machines. They are *improved* each year because the dream of perfection is a feasible one. Striving for an orderly language gives us law, blueprints, measurements. We should obviously aim to express ourselves in refined laws and sentences. But a machine does not run if it's incomplete. Its perfection is closely related to its completeness. That might be true for math, but it ain't true for language. Even if Mary agreed language is more organism than mechanism, she would have disagreed for the hell of it. In subtle as well as explicit ways she had been flirting with me. I decided it was a test. We decided to become friends. The next morning she sat with me and my tape recorder at the Syracuse airport. There was snow on the tarmac. I told her I wanted to interview her about Etheridge Knight. She said yes immediately. She was an amazing storyteller. When we talked of the years she was Etheridge Knight's student in Minneapolis, she told me about the time she babysat for him and Mary McAnally. The house was full of poets: Denise Levertov, Quincy Troupe, James Wright. She made chili for the children, a boy they named Etheridge Bambata and a girl they named Mary Tandiwie. While she stood in the kitchen that night, a famous, handsome white poet showed her his penis. As thick and freckled as a trout, if you can imagine, she said with her eyes cocked. She asked me to keep his name a secret. It's not here in the story she told me about her adventures with Etheridge Knight:

> I guess I was twenty. It was 1975, I was living with the prettiest man you
> ever saw. He wound up married to the Clinique girl making like a zillion
> dollars to fucking model. And I went to a poetry reading. I'd read
> Etheridge. He'd had a poem, I think "Hard Rock," in the Norton anthol-
> ogy. Either "Hard Rock" or "The Idea of Ancestry." And I went to hear

him read and I was just knocked out. I mean you have to understand things that just weren't as common then. I had been brought up in this small Texas town, I hung out around a lot of redneck storytellers. My father was a great barroom storyteller. He liked to gamble and I realized, early on, the advantage of telling stories as a way to keep people from kicking your ass. Especially if you took their money. And to meet some brothers in college, but you just gotta understand how segregated things were. Until I got to college it was almost not possible to have friends of different colors. My mother marched with Dr. King in Selma, Alabama. My father was the only guy I knew who had a black friend. The only white guy I knew [with a black friend], and he'd known him since he was a kid. But I remember in 1971 reading Maya Angelou's *Caged Bird*. I'd read the *New Yorker* at the library. I'd read poems mostly because I wanted to be a poet and it was all James Merrill and Bishop and stories by John Cheever and then reading *Caged Bird*. I remember saying to my mother, *I didn't know you could write about this*. And then when I saw Etheridge get up and profess. He'd just moved there with Mary McAnally and they'd adopted these two kids, a little boy and a girl, and Mary was this white woman from Oklahoma, very southern. I went to see him read and it was the same feeling I had with Maya Angelou. I didn't know you—he also did "Shine," which was something I had heard orally. An oral tradition and an oral art was a lot of what he talked about as a teacher. [His teaching] was one of those deals where you'd pay Etheridge and you'd go meet at his house once a week. It was him and Robert Bly came maybe a quarter of the time. And Audre came. You gotta imagine twelve or fifteen people in this house in Minneapolis and it's 30 below outside and you're slow-dancing with Audre Lorde. He called it the Free People's Poetry Workshop. This is 1975. I think this was the earliest incarnation of it. In 1974, '75 there was something called the National Poetry Festival.

It happened in Michigan ... It was like every poet in America. Ferlinghetti was there. Bill Knott was there. I think I'd gone to hear Bill Knott. The second workshop, Bly came. Bly was translating Rilke then. Who I didn't like. I didn't understand it. It didn't have enough things in it. It didn't have enough of the world in it. It took me a long time; Hass had to teach me how to read that. Bly was talking about the Soul and the nature of the poet and the Soul. Stuff that actually now I kind of believe, but I remember saying to him—everybody was very reverent, and in the first workshop I kind of didn't say anything—I was the youngest one, I was twenty. David Wojahn was in this workshop. Bly was talking about the Soul and at the end of it I said, *Bullshit, I don't even think I have a fuckin' soul.* At which point Etheridge busted out laughing and he was like, "Oh Texas, you been sitting there with your mouth shut but it's all coming out now!" I felt very freed by him suddenly to write—I was writing so badly. He taught me about Gwendolyn Brooks. He showed me how to read Keats. He had this enormous knowledge of poetry from being in the joint. He loved Yeats. He quoted a lot of Yeats. He spent a lot of time professing and testifying. We would read everybody's poems, drink wine. I remember him being very generous with everybody ... You can't be a junkie that long and not know how to scam and know how to bob and weave and know how to duck your head and *aww shucks* and drag your toe and say, *I'm so sorry.* He had that blight of somebody who's been in the joint, who feels bad about himself. He had a great love of poetry as this grand Oz-like place, but he was kind of committed to go to [poetry] with his hat in his hand. In some ways he was a con about it. In some ways he knew it was a con. I mean you never saw him do a poem a different way. He knew which way it worked. He had a rap. He was really a politician. He was about bringing people together. He liked everybody to come over to the house and drink wine and stay up late. I remember my mother, who was then a fifty-five-year-old white woman, coming to visit me, and we went to a party and I'm looking for her and I walked outside and she's on the back porch smoking a joint with Etheridge. He's sitting there spread-legged and she stands up with a reefer in her hand and says, *I like Etheridge.*

LINE 32: SPLIT/MY GUTS

LINE 33: I HAD ALMOST
CAUGHT UP WITH ME

The giant many fans know as "Mega Tall Paul" was approximately half a century old the first time his father kissed him. Giants are difficult to kiss unless one is also a giant. As you know, Tall Paul towered in a realm of his own. The current *Guinness World Records* lists him as a clean eleven feet tall. He is in fact eleven foot, two and seven-eighths inches. After Tall Paul told a cashier, who'd asked his height, he was eleven feet, two and seven-eighths inches, she said with a frown, "Why you gotta add the *seven-eighths*, ain't eleven foot two already tall enough?" Tall Paul wanted to kiss her because no one else in all his years had ever told him it was a vain thing to say. He was well known for his large self-regard, but told the cashier he was only trying to sound exact. He wanted to kiss her for her illuminated critique, and if he had, it would have required severe bending. Mostly Tall Paul hugged people to his waist; he did not bend. Most of the fans who lined up to greet him after his shows were children. Mostly all he did was stand around. He poked his hands through the holes cut in the top of the circus tent when he raised his arms—a show highlight. Occasionally he wanted to kiss one of the lovely indifferent mothers of the children who were his fans. Sometimes he wanted to be kissed by one strange woman after another. He missed his wife. He was a passionate man. His shirt pits always had a kind of sweat-and-sugar smell to them. Occasionally he wanted one of the grown-up women to breathe his scent. Mostly all he did was stand around. His wife was not especially impressed. His mother, brother, and father were definitely his biggest fans. Tall Paul was glad he'd get to spend a couple of days with them in Florida. He wanted them to see how well he was doing. His extra-long shoes and clothes were tailor-made, he had been on the cover of a few little-read magazines devoted to freak fans. He was a minor celebrity, but no one needed to know who he was to gawk at his height. Three different security agents pulled him aside to take selfies at the airport when he landed. Sometimes he searched for images of himself posted on Instagram. Usually the picture was of some stranger wildly grinning beside his crotch. A few times it was just a shot of his nostrils and the bottom of his chin. When Tall Paul hugged people to his waist, it was not unlike the way his father and brother, two average-size black men, hugged people. His father and brother were military men. His father and brother were sports fans. His father and brother did not kiss each other upon greeting. Tall Paul had just about freaked out when a foreigner at one of his events decided, upon realizing he could not kiss Tall Paul on the cheek, kissed the gi-ant's large, narrow hand. Any kiss in the region of his waist, which was just about all kisses when they happened, made Tall Paul blush. One of the security guards, a fit Hispanic woman, taking a selfie with him at the airport kissed his hand. He got a slight erection. He thought of the woman's hair and mouth and breasts and ass along the entire cab ride to the home of his brother in Tampa. His brother, an average-size man, jumped from military aircrafts for a living. The giant liked to think it was because it gave his brother a view of his life. The giant suspected his brother was lonely falling from those heights. His brother's daughters met him at the door when he stooped, practically bowing as he entered the house. The daughters, giggling, seven and ten, hugged Tall Paul's kneecaps. He pulled two coins made of pure, 300-year-old silver from his pocket and passed one to each of them. He nodded toward the mother of the girls, his brother's wife, his sister-in-law. He wasn't sure what she thought of him. Tall Paul went down to his knee and kissed his mother. She had been waiting to kiss him. He had flown several hours from a land of twelve-month snows into a land of 24-hour humidity. She would never tell him whether he smelled unpleasant. He kissed her on her jaw; she kissed him on the cheek. Then as the giant's father half-hugged him, the giant accidentally, almost automatically kissed his father on the cheek. It was a peck really, distributed closer to his ear than his cheek, burning imperceptibly as they pulled apart. A blush of silence opened, for a moment, between them. Even if the giant had not been a giant, he would have known, as all average boys know, boys do not kiss men; men do not kiss. The summer Tall Paul was sixteen, for example, before his father left for Korea, his father told him he'd be the big man of the house and shook his hand. When his father returned a year later, he shook Tall Paul's bigger, longer hand in the same way, perhaps more firmly. Rarely has the giant kissed standing perfectly upright. When the time came to kiss his petite bride twenty years ago, he fell to a knee, lifted the veil, and leaned into the soft clearing between her ear and shoulder blade, kissed her neck. He did not kiss his father the day of the marriage despite the wide smile they shared. In Florida when the giant's father embraced him, he could not ever recall a time they'd been that close. Without thinking, he kissed the side of his father's face. The kiss was so near his ear, the giant could have whispered something about sadness to him. They pretended it had not happened.

But that is not the story I intended to tell. I intended to tell you about the first time my father kissed me. The storyteller always tells his own story. All fables tell the storyteller's story. When I am having trouble saying what I want to say, I turn to the fable, just as Etheridge Knight did. The story entitled "A Fable"—for his adopted son, Etheridge Bambata, and his adopted daughter, Mary Tandiwie—is about seven men and women "in prison because their skins were black." The prisoners paced their cells strategizing the best way to get out of prison. They never escaped. "Rehabilitation & Treatment in the Prisons of America" is a dark fable wherein a convict "strolled into the prison administration building to get assistance and counseling for his personal problems." He walked continuously through dialectical doors. When he came to Custody and Treatment, he chose Treatment, went in, and was confronted with two more doors: First Offender and Previous Offender. Again he chose the proper door and was confronted with two *more* doors. After several more doors the convict came finally to two doors marked: "Black and White. He was Black, so he rushed—*ran*—through that door—and fell nine stories to the street." "I had almost caught up with me," Knight writes in "The Idea of Ancestry." This is the story he tells of himself, the son entering doors in search of a better version of himself. The storyteller always tells his own story. The future Etheridge Knight biographer will simultaneously write an autobiography. Fathers who go missing and fathers who are distant will become the bones of the stories. There will be a fable about a giant who grew too tall to be kissed by his father. My father must have kissed me when

139

I was boy. I can't really say. I was taught as all boys are taught: boys should not be kissed; men do not kiss. By the time I was eleven or even ten years old I was as tall as him. I was six inches taller than him by the time I was fifteen. My biography about Knight would be about intimacy, heartache. While I was writing about him spiraling through middle-age, the thing I feared most happened: I became a middle-aged cliché. Consumed by the ways my parents damaged me. Insecure, reckless, lonely, a strange voice echoing in a giant helmet.

I'd taken a plane to my brother's home in Tampa so the four of us could drive the two hundred or so miles to Miami to see the Dolphins, my father's favorite NFL team, play the Giants, my brother's favorite team. During the drive, my mother asked why I wasn't wearing my wedding ring. Whatever I told her, she accepted for the time being. Or she was thinking, "I can't believe you kissed your father." Everyone fell silent when it happened. My father didn't quite look me in the face. My brother slapped his hands and said something about the football game. My father wore his Dolphins jersey, my brother his Giants cap. My mother and I were dressed like civilians at the game. It occurred to me the men wore face masks perhaps to avoid kissing. The Giants won by two touchdowns. My brother teased my father, poking him in the ribs before patting him on the back. Just as we began climbing the stadium stairs, a cussing ruckus broke out between two drunk white men several rows below. A tattooed muscular man swung almost gleefully in the direction of a smaller man who ducked and dodged, swinging in retreat. After a few hot moments, they quit, as if realizing we bystanders would not intervene. My mother reprimanded the security guard who'd watched like the rest of us as the two men flailed, failing to land a single blow. We had two separate rooms at a hotel across from the airport. I'd have to catch a plane out of Miami early the next morning. My mother brought over two small cups of some kind of peach-flavored schnapps, glancing once more at my bare ring finger before exiting. My brother and I stayed up late talking. The next morning, before heading to the airport—I meant to wait until the last minute—my brother and I went to our parents' hotel room. I'd had a dream the night before. The four of us were seated in the stadium. From behind me I could hear someone saying, "Don't you come nowhere near my grave! Don't you come nowhere near my grave!" That's pretty much all that happened. The men we'd seen fighting at the end of the game did not appear in the dream. The stands sloped into oblivion. They were full of stadium trash, but they were empty. I didn't tell anyone about it. I almost mentioned it in the hotel room when my mother shook her head mumbling something about a premonition. They had slept separately in the room's double beds. For some reason my mother had made her bed. Flowers were printed on her new pajamas. Her hair was immaculate. I have never seen her tend to her hair, but I have never seen a hair out of place. When I kissed her on the top of her forehead, she smiled just as her granddaughters had when I kissed them the day before. My father sat on the bed with tears on his face. I had seen him weep at his mother's funeral; I had heard him crying on the other side of a door the year he and my mother came close to divorce, but I had never seen him sob the way he did that morning, when I told him my marriage was ending. I can't describe it, the gentleness. It shocked us, my brother, mother, and me. No one said anything. Then he rose and embraced me for what felt like two or three minutes. My face was against his shoulder. Before letting go, he kissed me, quickly, softly.

LINE 35: DAMMING

MY STREAM

THE BLUE ETHERIDGE

Dear Parole Board of the Perennial Now,
let me begin by saying it's very likely
none of my ex-wives will vouch for me.
Let's just say the parable
of the Negro who uses his dick for a cane
and the parable of the Negro who uses his cane
for a dick convey the same message to me.
I'm sorry. You mean before that?
Well, it's as if some ghost the height
of my granddaddy was lighting a cigarette
the wrong way to symbolize my muddy path
through life. You ever seen the Mississippi?
You'll learn all you need to know
if you look at the wall of my kinfolk's pictures.
Belzora. BuShie. My sisters. Me
and my brothers fishing in high waters.
Whenever I see brown hills and red gullies,
I remember what the world was like

before I twisted spoons over flames.
I pissed from a bridge the day I left.
Yes Sir, I've changed, I've changed.
But I won't be telling you the story
of the forlorn Negro or the Negro cutthroat
or the Negro Hero or the Negro Tom.
I won't be telling you the story of the night
I died. I believe everything comes back
to music or money. Belly Song.
Song of the twelve-fingered fix.
Song of The Gemini Women. I know I'm cursed.
I sang out to the Baptists I saw gathered
on the riverbank the day I left. I sang out
to the reeds straight as tongues and the salmon
in the waters of my people, and beyond that
to my barrel-backed shadow damming the stream.

LINE 36: MY GENES

I.

"The Idea of Ancestry" was among the first poems to put before me the question of my own idea of ancestry. When I tried a similar familial inventory, I could come up with only a dozen or so names: 1 grandmother, 1 mother, 1 half aunt, 2 half uncles (1 dead), a handful of half cousins, a half brother, a stepfather. My younger brother, James L. Hayes II, has my father's name because James L. Hayes is, biologically speaking, not my father. For years, whenever I asked my mother about it she'd respond, "You got a father." Moreover, as far as she was concerned, I have more of a father than she or her three siblings, each with a different father, ever had. Sometimes you have to conjure an idea of ancestry, an idea of family. But I was beginning to feel like all my poems were obsessed with questions of fatherhood, manhood, brotherhood. So long as I didn't know who my real father was, I feared I'd be writing, obsessing, over the same theme. As this book suggests, my obsessions have endured. My obsessions have morphed into a kind of life's work. In any case, in 2003, just after my son was born, I asked my mother again: Who is my father? To my surprise she gave me my biological father's name.

When I met Earthell "Butch" Tyler Jr. for the first time, in February 2004, he did not begin by telling me the year he was born or the names of his siblings and his mother. He told me his daddy, my grandfather, was a war hero. Earthell Tyler Sr. had been killed saving another soldier's life in Vietnam. "There were medals to prove it," Butch said. A Purple Heart and a Bronze Star. He promised to find them and show me. I'd traveled 500 miles from Pittsburgh, Pennsylvania, the place I lived, to Columbia, South Carolina, the place I was born. I'd traveled thirty-two years as the son of James L. Hayes, the man who'd raised me, to find Butch, the man whose blood ran through me.

"I don't want anything. I only want to look into your face," I said to Butch when I spoke to him on the phone for the first time. His voice warm, already familiar, he said he wanted to meet me as soon as possible. That evening I followed the address he gave me to a run-down neighborhood some people called "The Hole." At the edge of the road behind me two or three boys played basketball in the darkness, and beyond them, fifteen minutes deeper into Columbia, my mother sat trying to imagine this meeting.

"Lord, he look just like you!" Butch's girlfriend Ronnie said when she opened the door. He and his oldest son were living in Ronnie's tiny apartment with her and her children.

"Come here and let me look at you." Butch gestured through a gauze of cigarette smoke. "You definitely got the Tyler head," he said when I sat across from him at a small dining-room table. He stubbed his cigarette and pulled a crumpled pack from the pocket of his short-sleeve work shirt. His arms were long and muscled. He had the leanness of an athlete, but the wear in his face revealed the physical labor that kept him lean.

"You got the Tyler head," he said again, suddenly palming my head. "You got it just like me and your granddaddy got it." He took out his wallet and carefully removed a worn, black-and-white photograph only a little bigger than a stamp. Peering into it I saw a head the size of a thumbprint. It was so faded, I could barely make out the man's features. Butch insisted he looked just like us. I need only look in the mirror to see it. And it might have been true. For months after that visit, when I tried to remember what Butch looked like, I could recall nothing but a darker version of my own face; when I tried to remember the photograph, I could recall nothing but shadow.

Before his sister Maimie told him about me, Butch had had no idea I walked the earth. She'd helped me find him, although when my mother first put us in contact, Maimie said she had not seen Butch for at least a year. Since his divorce he'd been wandering between women, she said. But he was a good man. Good with his hands; he could fix all sorts of machines. She said he might have been an artist, a poet like me, had he not dropped out of school to help raise his brothers and sisters. I heard, too, that he was left-handed; that there was a mole on his forehead in exactly the same place as the mole on mine. But that wasn't true. Butch and Maimie barely knew each other, in fact. She had not been raised in the same house as him. They shared the same last name, but Earthell Tyler Sr. had not been her father. At first I'd thought she was keeping him from me. Or perhaps from my mother. How could a sister not know where her own brother was living? But after two months of searching, she found Butch and called me with his phone number.

The night I met Butch I could barely see the tall sixteen- or seventeen-year-old in the Polaroid I'd stolen years earlier from my mother's old photo album. The face had aged, but the hand moving between a can of beer and a cigarette was the same big hand I'd seen resting on my mother's small shoulder. Scribbled on the back of the picture in my

mother's handwriting: "Butch and Me at the El Matador Bay somewhere dancing around. We had a boss time! February 19, 1971." The
date was five years after his father had died in Vietnam, November 17,
1965, and almost nine months to the day before my birth on November
18, 1971.

"I remember that night," Butch smiled when I told him about the
photograph. "I got so drunk your momma had to drive. She didn't even
have her license yet. She swerved so much I got sick, but we made it to
a hotel not far from the club."

I knew this story. The story my mother told me to explain why she'd
never told me about Butch. I was waiting to see how he'd finish it.

"Your momma's always been a little crazy, but I really loved her back
then. She was my first love and I think I was hers." He took a drag from
his cigarette, thinking. "That's why I can't figure out why the hell she
ain't tell me about you?" he said, half asking, half fussing. He seemed
to have no idea anything wrong might have happened that night.

"I don't know. You'll have to ask her," I said to Butch, looking away
from him. My mother had told me they'd fought in the hotel. "We
fought and he took it," she said the day I'd called to ask her whether
Butch, the boy in the Polaroid, was my father. "I guess nowadays they
call it rape . . . I was too embarrassed to tell anybody I was pregnant.
Definitely not him and his mother, Miss Rebecca. When she died, it
was the thing I regretted most."

I felt like a coward for not asking him, was what my mother told me
true? Or maybe I felt it would be wrong to accuse him. But, really, it
was why I'd come. Had I been born as a result of rape? What did that
say about who I was; about the kind of blood that made me? I had to
see the man to know the truth. And sitting across from him I still didn't

147

know. I strained to see the person he might have been beneath the person he seemed to be. Perhaps my mother had said it to protect herself. Maybe she was unsure. A minute after telling me who my father was and what he'd done, she was reminiscing about him; she was promising to help me find him; asking did I want her there when I met him; apologizing for keeping me from my kin. Having told me the thing she thought she would take to her grave—not that she'd been raped, but that I was his son—she talked, as she rarely did, about what it had been like growing up. How poor she and her sister and two brothers were, raised by a single mother.

"They call the kind of place we lived the projects now. It was the projects then, just a little newer. I can remember thinking Butch's family got rich when his father died in the war. I would sit on my steps across the street from their house, and watch all those kids opening sodas and then leaving the half-full cans on the porch. I wanted to be part of their family. Miss Rebecca had a lot of kids and I became her babysitter."

In the photograph, they clutch each other at the waist. The thick veins looping Butch's hands and forearms are like my own. With his soft, crooked afro and big eyeglasses, he looks incapable of violence. I know that's a foolish thing to say. Maybe a son with no father is capable of anything. This is one of the stories I've told myself. If a boy's father died, he might drop out of school, as Butch did, to take care of his mother and siblings. Brokenhearted, he might begin drinking; he might get drunk enough to hurt and forget. And I've told myself that a daughter raised with no father, as my mother was, might also be capable of anything. If her father was absent, five states north with his legitimate wife and children, she might fall in love with all the wrong men. She might hurt and forget. I have been thinking about what the two of them, Butch and Ethel, have in common and what I have in common with them. I want to say it's that we come from a long line of fatherless sons and daughters; that with our pruned and truncated and broken-limbed family trees, we are like so many rootless African-American people of the Diaspora. But such social theories never explain enough. History develops its own mythology.

"My son Earthell Number 3 got his momma's head, but his little brother, Rashad, your little brother, Rashad, he got our head," Butch said. He called for Earthell Number 3 to come out and meet his brother. Twenty or twenty-one years old, he emerged from a back room talking on a cellphone. With his outsized jersey, loose jeans, and ball cap, he was good-looking with a sort of serious friendliness, a cool warmth. Maybe it didn't surprise him that his father might have a son he didn't know about.

"What up, big brother," he said as he put his long arms around me.

Ronnie asked us to stand side by side. I am six foot five and he was an inch or two taller than me. An inch or two shorter than me, Butch stood grinning at us.

"Damn, y'all tall," Ronnie said. "He definitely your son, Butch."

"You want me to pick up some more beer, Pop?" said Earthell #3 looking, I think, for a way to get back out of the room. I wondered why he lived with Butch while his brother, Rashad, stayed with their mother.

"Hell yeah, baby! Earthell," he exclaimed, grabbing the boy's shoulder as he looked at me, "Earthell is my partner!"

"Your daddy likes to drink," Ronnie said. "Too much."

It's not that it felt wrong to have her call him "my daddy." It's how easily she—all of them—seemed to accept me. I'd arrived in my mother's Volvo, the car that is an emblem of the most stuck-up members of the black middle class. I'd flown down in the middle of the week from my job as a college professor. I'd entered their home wearing the long, black coat my mother called "nice and expensive." Next to Earthell III, my new half brother, I felt I was wearing the wrong skin. But they'd welcomed me in. Butch was calling me "son" before the car's engine cooled.

2.

Nearly two years later, in January 2006, I spoke with Butch in person again for only the third time. I wanted to know more about my blood, my grandfather, our history. What was his earliest memory of his father? I wanted him to describe the last time he'd seen him; what he remembered about the day he learned his father was dead. I wanted to know how it changed the family. Butch had moved two or three times since I'd last seen him. He was renting a room in a motel off the highway. He had a new job out of town doing construction work. He no longer lived with Ronnie—kicked out, I assumed, because of his drinking—but he asked me to meet him at her place. I hoped to catch him that night before he was drunk.

"My daddy didn't give a fuck!" Butch said half slouched at the table, a beer in hand, a cigarette between his lips. I knew there should have been only the two of us, but I could tell he didn't want me to see where he lived. We sat drinking with Ronnie and her best friend, Brenda. Ronnie's ten-year-old son watched two older boys play a video game, their taunts and laughter blending with the sound of "What's Going On"—Marvin calling, "Brother, Brother, Brother," from a tiny radio.

I propped a tape recorder in the middle of the table, hoping Butch's voice would cut through the noise. He was talking to me, but he was talking to Ronnie as well, half boasting, half testifying when I asked him his earliest memory of his father.

"You know what? He didn't give a fuck," Butch said to the room. "When he came back home and Mother had all those children, you know what he said? 'How y'all doing?'"

The boys playing the video game let out a snatch of laughter.

"Don't use that kind of language on the tape!" Brenda said, Ronnie nodding.

"It's alright," I said beginning to realize how difficult this interview might be. Difficult for me to moderate; difficult for Butch to recall. "You mean he was easygoing?"

"Yeah, he didn't give a fuck."

"Was it that he didn't give a fuck or was it that he was easygoing?" I said. "There's a difference."

"He was easygoing," said Butch, beginning to soften. "He was like me. When he came home—he didn't come home that much—when he came home everybody would say: 'Earthell's home! The man!'"

"He was in Korea, too, right?" I said only a little surprised at how suddenly he seemed to be opening up. He could be, at times, the most forthcoming man I've ever met. Gentle and charming. When I'd told him I wanted to interview him about his father, he seemed ready to tell me every story right there over the phone. When he said his father served in Korea, it prompted a slightly different version of the man. Not a man green to war when he went to Vietnam, but someone experienced, a career soldier. Now I wanted to know any stories about the army—about being a black man in the army.

"Yeah, he served a year in Korea. But he never was home. He never was. You know why? My momma wasn't about that. She could have been with him; I could have been with him. Every time he left, we could have went with him. But she wouldn't do it. She wasn't willing to leave home."

"'Cause she was a strong woman," Brenda said, but Butch was paying no attention, speaking almost to himself. Ronnie was looking lovingly from Butch's face to mine. Maybe she'd heard some of it before, but I don't think she'd ever seen Butch reminiscing this deeply.

"Before he went to Vietnam, he came home. For a minute. He never was there. He came home in a VW. He had a red Volkswagen. He came home . . . He said, 'Well, I'm going to Vietnam.' I think he knew he wasn't coming back. Me, my momma, my oldest brother, Darrel, and one of Pop's drinking partners—'cause Pop liked to drink, too—one of his drinking partners drove us to Alabama. And he was going to leave Alabama and go to Vietnam. Before that he came home. And he left the VW to Darrel. Now Darrel wasn't his son! When they got married, Mother already had Darrel. He left his red Volkswagen to Darrel because he was the oldest. *Whose* he was didn't matter to him. 'Cause that's how my daddy was. Darrel was a Tyler and that's just how he looked at it. After that he went to Vietnam. If he had made it back, he would have retired. But he didn't make it back. And he died trying to save somebody else."

"Do you know what happened? Who he saved, how he died?"

"Well, they sent us the Purple Heart and the Bronze Star. I saw the official papers that said Sergeant Earthell Tyler did such and such and such. That's why they awarded him the Bronze Star."

"You could probably get that information from the government,"

Brenda said. "You're a journalist, I bet they'd give that information to you."

"He's his grandson, he's family," Ronnie added. "They have to give him that information."

But I'm not a journalist, I'm a poet. I'm not good at asking questions; I'm good at making things up. What I wanted to know, Butch couldn't tell me. I had not gone to Washington to see his father's name etched into the black stone, but I'd seen it online: Panel 3 East, Row 96. The only "Earthell" among the 58,286 names, he had been easy to find. "Earthell" sounded both strange and familiar to me; it seemed grand and simple at the same time. It sounded like the kind of name that required a nickname. He might have been called "Slim" or even "Bullethead," nicknames I had growing up. He might have been the original "Butch." (I had not thought to ask Butch how he came by the name.) In the army they might simply have called him Tyler or Sarge. Among websites devoted to veterans, I found the slim details of his life: E5, US Army, age 35, married, Delta company, 2nd Battalion, 7th Cavalry, born July 22, 1930, died November 17, 1965, cause of death: small arms fire.

It was online that I learned he was among those killed during three days of fighting in the Battle of Ia Drang, the first major battle between the United States Army and the People's Army of Vietnam (PAVN). I had not heard of the battle until I saw his name associated with it, but there were detailed accounts of it on websites throughout the Internet. From the US Army's website I learned that it was the first battle in which US forces combined air mobility and air artillery. There were almost no roads into the area, but the new airmobile tactics allowed soldiers on their way to battle and soldiers wounded and killed in battle to be transported to landing zones by Huey helicopters. It was also the battle in which the PAVN and Viet Cong forces learned that they could undermine the air strikes by fighting at very close range. They would later refine this tactic, calling it "getting between the enemy and his belt." Many websites featured animated maps and diagrams that reduced the battle and landing zones to the kinds of lines and arrows you might find in a football coach's playbook. At weweresoldiers.net images of the helicopters and soldiers were being sold for as much as 350 dollars. At juniorgeneral.org there was even a war game, complete with military figurines and a game board. I began to see the mythic proportions the battle had acquired in the forty-plus years since it had happened. At lzxray.com I learned of Lieutenant General Hal Moore, whose book about the battle, *We Were Soldiers Once . . . and Young: Ia Drang—The Battle That Changed the War in Vietnam,* was made into a film starring Mel Gibson in 2002. The yellow-haired Moore was mentioned on Wikipedia in relation to the yellow-haired Lieutenant Colonel George Armstrong Custer, who commanded the same unit, the 7th Cavalry, in the infamous Battle of the Little Bighorn in 1876. There were other parallels between the two battles: the underestimation of the enemy, the perils facing outnumbered American forces in unfamiliar terrain. The Ia Drang campaign is described as two fights between November 14 and November 17: the first at landing zone X-ray, the second near the smaller landing zone Albany. I wondered if Butch's father, my grandfather, was among the 2nd Battalion, 7th Cavalry ambushed by PAVN forces near landing zone Albany. According to the synopsis, the fighting was "a wild mêlée, a shoot-out, with the gunfighters killing not only the enemy but sometimes their friends just a few feet away." The landing zone Albany battle lasted through the day and night, descending into hand-to-hand combat. My grandfather was among the more than 155 killed and 126 wounded on November 17, the deadliest day for American forces during the entire Vietnam War. I wondered what he'd done to earn the medals. I searched for his name on the sites by and for veterans: sites memorializing little-known fallen soldiers. There were ardent testimonies and words such as *hero*, *honor*, *sacrifice* floating against backdrops of American flags and photos of young men, but on the rare occasion Earthell Tyler was mentioned, it was as a name among the dead. Big or small, war or warrior, every website was steeped in prideful nostalgia. None of them told me what I wanted to know. I knew Sergeant Earthell Tyler died in the Battle of Ia Drang and was decorated for bravery and service, but I did not know what he'd done there. I knew he was a man whose head was shaped like mine, but I did not who he was: whether he was a prankster or preacher, whether he sang out loud or to himself, whether he thought of his fellow soldiers or his family in the moments before his death.

"What did she do when she found out he was gone? When she found out he'd been killed?"

"I'll never forget that day. A taxicab driver brought the telegram to the house. I'll never forget that day," Butch said as he lit another cigarette. "I was right there. I was surprised she broke down like she did. I didn't really think she loved my daddy. But uh, I was so surprised that she broke down and she cried."

"How old were you?" I said, already imagining a boy shocked to see his mother crying for the first time. Maybe more shocked by the sight of her weeping, than at the news of his father's death, at first. I could see Rebecca Tyler now, and I could hear the big sound of her weeping. And the softness of it.

"I was eleven or twelve. I remember when the taxicab driver brought that telegram."

"I need details," I said, hoping to coax him into a deeper story, something better than my imagination. "Was it a weekend? Were you coming home from school? Were you watching cartoons? Was your mother at work?"

"I think *I* was at work." He laughed. "I've been working ever since I was twelve. I had a job changing tires."

"You were pretty much taking care of the family while he was gone?"

"Yeah, my great-uncle got me a job changing tires." I could see Butch kneeling at a car in 1965, a boy whose body was being trained already in the habits of work. Except it occurred to me that he was already working even before his father was killed. He had not gone to work to take his dead father's place as breadwinner, like some character in a Charles Dickens novel. What I'd been thinking when I came to speak with Butch was too easy. I thought if he'd never lost his father, he might never have lost his family. I thought he would never have started drinking, might have learned to love my mother the right way. But the truth was more layered: the shadow of the life he had turned from, or been forced to turn from, covering the life he lived.

I said, "So you didn't think they loved each other?" realizing, too, the story I expected to hear about Earthell Tyler Sr. was too easy. I'd imagined the words he'd written home to his wife. I'd believed he was a man with a deep, almost foolish capacity for love—a man capable of loving even a country or woman that might not love him back. His love was so vast he believed anyone could be changed by it: that a country which did not see his race as equal could be changed if he devoted his life to protecting it; that a woman could be changed by his devotion and give the same devotion back. But that was all too simple.

"When they got married, they were in love," Butch said. "Mother met my daddy when they were teenagers. She'd already had Darrel. They were young. Daddy was in the army. I think the problem was when she didn't want to go where he had to go. She just wasn't leaving her family to go to Europe or overseas or Germany—all them places he was going. She said, 'I just can't do that, Baby, I'm so sorry.' So he went by himself. Which was a problem. You can't leave your woman like that. That creates some problems."

Ronnie and Brenda and I, we all nodded at his words. His story reminded me of my own. Like Earthell Tyler Sr., James L. Hayes was a career military man; a black sergeant in the army. And like Miss Rebecca, my mother chose to stay in Columbia the years he was stationed on military bases inside and outside the country. He was called to Germany when I was eight and did not live in Columbia again "full-time" until he retired, fourteen years later. It was during those years I first remember meeting Miss Rebecca. She was tall, stern. Whenever we went to visit her, we'd sit quietly for hours in her den. Maybe there were photographs of her sons, daughters, and grandchildren all over the room. My mother told me babysitting for Miss Rebecca had been her first job, and I am thinking now that there was almost a kind of employer and employee formality between them. Something like respectful fear or fearful respect emanated from my mother in the woman's presence. Maybe during one of those visits she asked Miss Rebecca whether she should take the family abroad with James. Maybe Miss Rebecca told her not to follow him, just as she had not followed Earthell. "It's better to raise your children around their blood," she might have said. "They should grow up in a real neighborhood, not on military bases." These are the words I remember hearing when my father left for Germany. Maybe Miss Rebecca told my mother staying was the best way to have a stable family. Except none of it happened that way. As Butch said, leaving your woman behind created some problems.

There was a little rush of movement. The boys left the room. Brenda rose to leave. More than an hour had passed, but Butch and I were still where we'd started.

"But you know what," he said. "I'll say this much about him. He wasn't even in the United States and she was having babies. And she named every damn one of them Tyler. And you know what he said? Nothing. When he would come home—before he died he came back to the United States—you know what he said? Nothing. But I be the only Earthell Tyler Jr., Baby! My daddy the only man she ever married. I ain't no bastard. I ain't worried about it. My father was genuine."

He stood up smiling. "You know what I'm saying, Baby?" he sang leaning over to palm my head. "That's why you who you are! You got Tyler blood in you. You ain't no bastard, Baby. You be legit." He swaggered, staggered into the kitchen for more beer.

I've been thinking about the idea of legitimacy. Butch was one of eight or nine children—I never really got a clear number. He had not seen most of them since his mother's funeral six years earlier. All of them were scattered across the city. His emphasis on being legit, genuine, made me think he'd grown up believing he was more legitimate than any of his siblings. He was the only one born into a genuine family: a mother and father who were married. Except his siblings might have seen more of their fathers than he could see of his own. As one of the oldest children, he might have seen those men about his mother's house after his father died. Maybe before. I've been wondering whether he called any of those men *father*, if he ever wanted to call any of them father.

I did not think of myself as illegitimate, even when I knew James L. Hayes was not my biological father. I thought of him as my dad anyway. I grew old enough to catch the lies my parents told their friends who marveled at my height: to some they said it came from James's side of the family, to others my mother's. I grew old enough to know I had no memories of James that preceded the birth of my younger brother, old enough to wonder why my younger brother was named James L. Hayes II and not me. Perhaps I had not known what the word *father* meant. For a child, family and love have nothing to do with blood. My parents knew I'd figured it out, but for a long time none of us said anything. When my mother finally told me the truth, when I was eighteen, it was but a flash of admission. A nod passed between us and a moment later I was calling him father, she was calling him my father again. As a grown man, I did not want to find a father to replace James L. Hayes. I did not want a new name, but I wanted to know my family history. I believed knowing it could tell me not just who my people were but also who my children would be. Maybe Butch knew what I wanted, what I'd come looking for. He wanted to give me something to be proud of. The only thing he could offer was his father's story.

James L. Hayes had wanted to give me something else. A man who talked little of the past, he wanted to give his family a future to be proud of. An only child, he'd been born to a fourteen-year-old in Pompano Beach, Florida. He did not discuss the circumstances of his conception, but my mother told me his father had been an older man. He never knew him. He'd grown up shuffled between relatives. My mother told me how hard he'd had it, how poor and virtually parentless he'd been. She told me more than once how he never bothered looking for his father. I think now she was trying to tell me how much our lives were alike. He'd dropped out of high school and joined the army as soon as he was old enough to enlist. He'd been a private at Fort Jackson, Columbia, South Carolina, when he met her. They married when I was three. A year later my brother was born in Fort Bragg, North Carolina, during the brief period my mother followed him—though it was just a little ways from Columbia: we moved three hours away to North Carolina, then an hour away to Greenville, South Carolina. When my father was to be stationed in Germany, she moved back to her hometown, my brother and me in tow.

During the decades my father did not live in the house with us, he remained for me the man I'd thought he was when I was eight: an artist whose half-finished paint-by-numbers portrait of John F. Kennedy awaited him in the hallway; a music lover who left his Curtis Mayfield and Roberta Flack records behind for me; and above all a true soldier, a man of honor. I'd once seen him collar a young white private for strolling through an amusement park with the shirt of his uniform untucked. I'd watched with a mix of fear and awe as the white boy straightened himself up and then saluted my father. I can remember how broadly my mother smiled at the scene. In many ways he was always attentive, responsible, during those years, sending my mother money, sending my brother and me clothes and souvenirs from abroad (gaudy mugs from Germany when I was in the fourth grade, a jogging suit from Korea with my name stitched across the pocket when I was in the eighth grade), but he was mostly a husky, long-distance voice whose main refrain was, "Listen to your mother." He was her weapon. "I'm going to call your daddy" became a phrase very much like "I'm going to call the cops." He was too far to ever do anything, but her threat stilled me. As the man of the house in his absence, I wanted his respect. I never wanted to let him down.

By the time he retired and moved back to Columbia, though, the myths I'd made about him had clouded over. I wished the white boy he cornered at the amusement park had said: "I'm just here having a good time, man. Relax!" I was in my early twenties, measuring my idea of manhood against him. I saw him not as honorable but foolish, for remaining in the military—even for remaining married to my mother, and I often told my brother so. For a long time, I didn't think about how those years might have affected my little brother. He was just four when we moved to South Carolina, without our father, and eighteen, about to move from home, when our father retired. I doubt he remembers a time when the four of us lived together in the house. We spent summers, and often when our parents fought, weekends, in military quarters with our father the years he was stationed in Fort McClellan, Alabama. Our mother almost always stayed behind in Columbia. I remember the tanks and jets perched around the base like bland oversized toys, the distant camouflaged men. The military seemed a world of stale rituals and mindless regulations to me. It took my father, the hero, from his family. I had assumed my brother harbored the same kind of resentment for military life. Then he enlisted in the army. Ironically, he was sent to Fort Bragg, North Carolina, where he'd been born two decades earlier.

It broke my father's heart. "The military is no place for a black man," he told him. It shocked me to hear such a thing from a man who'd spent nearly half his life in the army. A man who'd been a leading army recruiter the years we lived in Greenville—in the same photo album in which I'd found the photo of Butch and my mother was a newspaper clipping of James receiving an award for his stellar recruiting record. I don't believe he lied to the poor black boys he talked into joining the army. He wanted to offer them the same kind of escape from poverty or rootlessness the army had given him. I think he believed there would never be anything his own sons would need to escape. "You're going to college," he often told us, but he never said how he would make it happen. There was no money, no knowledge of grants and fellowships. When I graduated from high school, I went to college on a basketball scholarship. I would not have gone otherwise. When my brother graduated four years later he was offered some partial academic grants, but not a full scholarship. He tried paying his way through college for a few semesters, but eventually decided—without discussing it with anyone in the family—that the best way to pay for school was to go into the military. It's a familiar story. When he retired after ten years in the army, he had a handful of college credits, but no degree. He'd been to Iraq and come home with bad knees.

Like my father, I was brokenhearted when my brother entered the military. Perhaps even more brokenhearted when he retired without fulfilling the dreams he'd had when he entered. I feared the military might make him into a dumb machine. I feared he might be ruined by learning to act without asking. But mostly I feared he'd come to have more in common with our father, with *his* father, than I did—that James L. Hayes would have more respect for the son who'd been a soldier. I have watched them, James L. Hayes the first and the second, standing side by side at the grill as if connected by something only they sense. And I have envied it. I've wondered how much of who my brother has become is the result of his blood history. I have watched them, father and son gesturing, laughing, as if they were the same person: the same gentleness and toughness, the same wide smile.

I believe our father returned home after retirement because of his *devotion*, which is a word like *love*, to his family. Or his devotion to the *idea* of family. And I want to say blind commitment to one's family is as dangerous as blind commitment to one's country, that sometimes it is more courageous to question or even abandon that which one loves. I'm not sure that's what I believe. Was Earthell Tyler Sr. blind? Was following an order the cause of his death? Was he like my brother and father, men devoted to words such as *duty* or *honor*, to ideas which can be held but never touched?

"Tell me something you remember about your father," I said when the room was quieter, just Ronnie, him, and me drinking and smoking, music from the 1970s still playing in the corner.

"I wasn't that close to him. I never really knew him." Butch lit another cigarette, calm enough to seem sober.

"But you wanted to know him."

"I really did. My mom wasn't that close to him, either. But he just wasn't there."

"Do you remember him making people laugh? Was he shy? Was he serious?"

"He was serious. But on the other hand, he was like me. He wasn't the kind of guy to kick the door in and shoot you for fucking his woman. He wasn't like that. He was a good guy. He died trying to save the life of one of the guys in his platoon. That's how he was."

"You never thought about going in the army?"

"I went in the army."

"You did? What happened? How old were you when you went in?"

"I was eighteen. And I had three kids. I had twins and a little girl. And I went in the army because I was trying to make it better for us. Everybody in my family was in the military. Your uncle Walter, your auntie Vickie. She was a lieutenant."

I should have asked whether he thought it was what his father had done or tried to do: make it better for all of them. The stories of young men who enter the army to better themselves are fairly common. Less common are the stories of men who enter the army to better their families. I should have been thinking again about the military as a vehicle of escape for black people. During Vietnam, America's army was more integrated than it had ever been. It meant something that Earthell Tyler was a sergeant, an E5, that the men he served and the men who served him were black and white. It meant something that James L. Hayes, who retired as an E9, would serve and be served in the same way. The leadership roles in the military have never been racially equal, but maybe in the midst of the Civil Rights Movement, the army was a model for America. Not because there was no racism, but because blacks and whites were willing, or forced, to crawl on their bellies together. Maybe the military was and is one of the few places minorities can ascend through service. As if proving a willingness to die for this country is the only way to get ahead if you cannot afford college. These are the things I thought later, and had I mentioned them then, maybe Butch would have told me how foolish I, someone who never entered the military, was for thinking them. At the time, though, all I could think about was his saying, "I had three kids."

"Where are these people?" I said. "How many damn brothers and sisters do I have?"

Butch let out a slightly embarrassed laugh.

"You know how many children your daddy got?" Ronnie said. "Seven."

"I went in the army for them," Butch continued. "I was going to marry my children's mother. Her name was Ella Mae. But it didn't work out. I hated the army. And I think the army hated me, too."

I should have been thinking about Butch in the military. He could have been in the same barracks as James L. Hayes at some point. I should have been thinking about how some black men seize upon the dream of America and some refuse it, how some embrace America for its rags-to-riches myths and others spurn this country because of its racist history. And how each kind of man is heroic in his attempt to define himself, be it through reason or passion, compliance or resistance, calm or outcry—how each of these desires can exist within the same man.

But I was calculating numbers in my head: Butch's three children by a woman named Ella Mae had to be just a few years younger than me; then came Earthell III, who was twenty-one; Rashad who was sixteen; I was the oldest of his children—it didn't add up to seven. I felt a web of siblings spreading around me. I might be related to half the people in Columbia, I thought. It was something I'd thought many times in the years before finding Butch.

"Did your father have brothers and sisters?"

"It was just him and his sister. There's a preacher in Denmark, South Carolina, right now. His name is Earthell Tyler. My daddy's sister named her firstborn son after her brother."

"What's her name?"

"I never met her. There are a lot of people I work with from Denmark, where he was born. There's a whole bunch of Tylers. The whole town is Tylers. But my daddy's uncle raised him and his sister here in Columbia. Uncle Johnny raised them. And every time I would see him—he was a deacon in the church, who raised my daddy—every time he would see me, he would say 'Oh my God' and kiss me on my forehead." Butch demonstrated by leaning to kiss me in the middle of my forehead. I could feel the wetness he left there like a small splatter of rain.

"Y'all gonna make me cry," Ronnie said over her beer. She was already crying.

"He loved my daddy just like that. He raised my daddy and his sister. That's all I know," he said leaning back in his chair. "I don't know their momma and I don't know their daddy. I know our people from Denmark. Every time he would see me: 'Look at that head. That's Earthell!' And he would kiss me. . . He used to kiss me. You come from a long line of men that love people. Alright. You come from a long line of loving men. Ain't nothing wrong with loving. That don't make you a punk. That makes you a man."

3.

During the flight back to Pittsburgh, I thought of the interview, how I'd failed at it; but more than that I thought of leaving Ronnie's place with Butch when we were done. I followed his swerving old pickup truck to his ex-wife's. She lived surprisingly close, but he'd visited so rarely, we got lost two or three times before we found it, an apartment dark enough to seem abandoned at the end of a long dirt driveway. Butch went to make sure it was the right place, and a few minutes later we stood on the unlit porch with Rashad Tyler: tall, quiet, sixteen, my little brother—the one Butch said was like me, like us.

What is that aura some boys have just before they grow into men?

Vulnerability? Openness? It was in Rashad, and it reminded me of the little brother I'd grown up with. It's the kind of goodness that makes certain boys perfect soldiers: makes them dutiful, makes them faithful. It's the kind of spirit that can be broken, or dulled with age.

"He think I don't love him," Butch joked, palming his son's do-ragged head. I could tell the boy smiled, but I couldn't make out his features in the darkness. We stayed only ten or fifteen minutes. I gave Rashad my phone number, told him to call if he ever needed anything. As we got ready to leave, Butch and I stepped from the shadows of the porch into the late, half-lit evening, and Rashad said, shyly: "You gone come see me, Daddy?"

It was the bond the three of us had in common: wanting to see and be seen by our father. Thinking about it on the plane home, I had to put my hand over my eyes. "Hell yeah, I'll see you, Baby," Butch said. It was nothing any of us believed.

■

Death breaks a man into sentences; it makes him as big and as small as a procession of words. And the words cast light on the body and the words cast shadows.

■

When a father is lost, the ones he leaves behind have to make everything up. The man must be set firmly upon the branch of his family tree, even if he seemed to speak little or have no history. Raised by his uncle Johnny in Columbia, kin to the black people of Denmark, let us make the father of Sergeant Earthell Tyler Sr. a farmer; let us make the sergeant's mother a tall brown woman with a love for gardening. Let the thing that separated the parents from their son and daughter, the crime against them or the crime they committed, the nature of the bad luck that befell them—let it remain a mystery.

When a soldier dies, especially in war, his loved ones make things up: even the past—which is not the same thing as history, the cool and generous spirit of the deceased, how he sent not only his family but also his sister and uncle Johnny money, how whatever child his wife bore while he was away became a member of his family. One must make up the secrets the wife never learned and the secrets the wife never shared. One must imagine the letters that arrived with hearts decorating her name and nicknames: Pussycat, Sugar Baby, Red Bone, Honey. One must make up the litany of promises and fantasies the man and woman could not keep.

When a loved one is lost, the ones left behind have to make up everything. I would like to make up my grandfather's future: imagine it beyond the years of service and medals of honor, and beyond the ensuing years he might have worked as a postman or prison guard. I imagine the way the bones of his huge fingers would begin to ache and give off, even forty years after the war, a vague gunpowder scent that only his eldest grandson could smell. If in his eighties he suffered some ailment that caused him to shrivel or dull, if he walked as humped as a walking cane or did not walk at all, I would be the one driving him to his doctor, clutching his arm at the car door, lifting him up.

■

Afterward, in a Pittsburgh bookstore I found, incredibly, my grandfather's name in *We Were Soldiers Once . . . and Young*. On page 261, when James H. Shadden recounts the battle, he says, "Men were wounded and dead," and among the last alive was Sergeant Earthell Tyler:

Tyler gave the only order I heard during the entire fight: "Try to pull back before they finish us off." . . . The five [of us] proceeded to try to pull back, but snipers were still in the trees. Soon I was hit in the right shoulder, which for a time rendered it useless. Tyler was hit in the neck about the same time; he died an arm's length of me, begging for the medic, Specialist 4 William Pleasant, who was already dead. . . . The last words Tyler ever spoke were "I'm dying."

I say, not "begging" for the medic but *asking*. Maybe *demanding*. He had led them through the jungle's foliage of noise, through the bullets and bodies of the enemy falling from the trees. He had led them until the trail vanished into the brush, the only one to say, "Try to pull back," when he saw the limbs of men and trees gouged by bullets. I had imagined him in death doing something unbelievable: jumping on a grenade to save his platoon, sacrificing himself. And reading the story and hearing the stories Butch told me, I still imagine him a hero, though not the kind the army had in mind. This man is my history. He and I, we see the blood on the deep, green leaves and we think the blood smells like gunpowder. We are not supposed to be there leading black and white boys down into the dirt. We are not supposed to be there with an ache blooming in our neck, spreading up to our ears and down into our body. We think calmly: *I am almost unborn.* I have made love to a woman and left her with a son who looks like me. I am not begging for the medic, I am asking if he is all right. I have a son who bears my name as if it were a long shadow, a glorious light. I am not dying.

LINE 37: ACROSS THE SPACE

In 2010, Fran Quinn casually asked if I was familiar with the poems of Christopher Gilbert. We were walking at the edge of a lake one night at Robert Bly's Great Mother Conference. I was there teaching a poetry workshop, but as the name implies (officially, the Great Mother and New Father Conference), it is far from your run-of-the-mill poetry gathering. There had been, since its 1975 inception, more than a few occasions for its poets, dancers, painters, storytellers, environmentalists, Jungians, tabla drummers, shamanic astrologers, and mythopoeticists to weep at the state of the cosmos or the sound of a sitar or the sight of the great Robert Bly crossing a rustic threshold. The kinds of people you rarely find at poetry retreats had taught there: Joseph Campbell, who wrote *The Hero with a Thousand Faces* and *The Power of Myth*, for example, and Marion Woodman, who co-wrote *Dancing in the Flames: The Dark Goddess in the Transformation of Consciousness*. The year I visited, Lewis Hyde was there. He wrote *Trickster Makes This World: Mischief, Myth, and Art*, and before that, *The Gift: Creativity and the Artist in the Modern World*, a landmark book about the importance of uncommodified art in a culture that means to commodify everything. As you might imagine from these titles, there were lots of mostly old men with beards, lots of mostly old women without bras, a few hippies with PhDs. But there was no television, no Internet, no easy escape route to town, and minus me, no black folk. I may have been only the third or fourth black dude to have ever attended.

White people shaking and hooting and fingering their chakras in the woods may sound, depending on your disposition, a little quaint or maybe a little dangerous, but this group was made of beautiful, expressive enthusiasm. Still, all through my time at the Great Mother Conference I pondered the ways it, like Cave Canem and Kundiman and CantoMundo, was a paradoxically open *and* closed community.

Whenever a white poet friend half-jokingly says, "I want to be the first white poet to teach at Cave Canem"—more than one or two have said it over the years—I feel the same mix of compassion and over-my-dead-body-ness. I have said once or twice over the years: "You should check out the Great Mother Conference."

Yes, Cave Canem has much to offer absolutely everyone; yes, people of color should, of all people, grasp the importance of integration and access. But I imagine the disconcerting self-consciousness these white friends would feel. It's not unlike the self-consciousness people of color feel pretty much everywhere, every day, I guess. I want for the poets outside of such "boutique retreats" what I want for the poets inside: a safe space, a space that permits transparency, risk, screwups, outrage, forgiveness, and genius. The success of such venues certainly suggests there are benefits to solidarity. Heaven has those pearly gates for a reason. FUBU is the official logo of Utopias everywhere: For Us, By Us. But I'm not advocating segregation so much as asking about our duties to the individuals who *could* but don't, or won't, belong to those communities. How should one balance the inclusiveness and exclusiveness of such spaces? Who should guard this balance, who should bridge it?

At the Great Mother Conference I was welcomed. I have not been back, but I felt welcomed. The participants, who understandably were eager to have a bit more youth and color, made every effort to bring me into their community. In fact, they sometimes seemed downright distracted by making me feel safe and welcomed. Fran, who had been at the Great Mother Conference since the very beginning, took me for walks. He talked about the future of the conference given its aging constituents. What would happen when the already-frail Bly grew too frail to attend? Fran could not have known his concerns for the future of that community made me think of the future of others. We talked often of Etheridge Knight, who'd attended the conference in its early years. We'd been talking about the joyous hell Knight had raised at this conference when Fran asked whether I knew Gilbert's work. Gilbert had driven Knight up to the Great Mother once. He'd co-founded the Worcester Free People's Artist Workshop with Knight in 1977, leading it from 1977 to 1981.

"He was a great poet, a black guy, a great guy," Fran said. Gilbert had published one book, *Across the Mutual Landscape*. There was a second book—maybe it was too political, too ahead of its time, Fran mused, but Chris had died in 2007, before it ever saw the light of day. Maybe Fran wiped his nose as he spoke, cleared his throat. I think he was always on the verge of tears that summer. Fran and the poet Mary Fell had been close friends of Gilbert and they now had the unpublished book back in Indiana. I didn't ask to see the manuscript, though Fran must have offered to send it to me. I told him I would run down *Across the Mutual Landscape* as soon as I was back home.

But what I did as soon as I was home was reacquaint myself with civilization, the Internet, my wife and my kids. Then a week or so after I'd been back, a friend, the poet Ed Pavlić, happened to e-mail me "Marking Time," a poem by Christopher Gilbert. Did I know the poem, he asked, assuming I already knew the poet.

I wrote back that I didn't know the poem. Was this Christopher

Gilbert deceased, I asked. "No, I'm pretty sure Chris Gilbert is alive and living in Providence," Ed replied, adding he'd been thinking about inviting him down to Georgia to read at his university. He wrote back a day later to say after some digging online, he discovered it was indeed the same Christopher Gilbert. His obituary says he died at fifty-seven on a Thursday in July 2007 at Rhode Island Hospital in Providence. That he was the husband of Barbara Morin, the father of Gracie Gilbert and Robin Gilbert, the stepfather of Heather Morin, a Professor of Psychology at Bristol Community College for fifteen years, and almost as an aside, "he was also a poet. His book of poems, *Across the Mutual Landscape*, won the 1983 Walt Whitman Award." Three years had passed since Gilbert's death, and there was still almost no word of it in the poetry community. Hearing about Gilbert suddenly from two different poets within a couple of weeks felt uncanny. Even more remarkably, Ed happened to be in Bloomington, Indiana, teaching at a writers' conference, about an hour from Indianapolis, where Fran lived. Ed had come across a copy of *Across the Mutual Landscape* in a Bloomington used bookstore. It was a book he'd always loved. I knew he'd be interested in the new work. Ed agreed to drive to Indy to get the posthumous manuscript from Fran. My acting as go-between was more a matter of curiosity than advocacy. Then *Across the Mutual Landscape* arrived in the mail.

During the one or two weeks it took Ed to get the unpublished collection back home to Georgia, scan it, and then e-mail that to me, I read and reread *Across the Mutual Landscape*. I was overwhelmed, awestruck, saddened. I was not yet sure what the later work would look like, but I was sure there was magic in the debut. I remember the first time I met my half brother, Earthell Tyler III. He was six eight, he looked more like my daughter than I do. That's the familiarity I felt reading *Across the Mutual Landscape.*

I was halfway through the book before I paused to write an exasperated e-mail to my poetry mentors, pals, and peers (especially my black poetry mentors, pals, and peers) asking what they knew of him and why those who knew his work had not told me about him. I e-mailed at least a dozen people "The Facts," the sixth and final section of Gilbert's long poem "Horizontal Cosmology." Here's how that poem opens:

> Looking down the empty Mason jars
> in the cupboard, I forget myself.
> I forget my name and its belongings.
> I forget my plastic ID card
> for the "Y," my Exxon credit card
> and the square feeling it leaves in my hand.
> I forget passing thirty and feeling nothing—
> but dreaming blue tears that night all the same.
> I forget wanting money, no, wanting
> to be like the men who have money,
> who piss against the wall of good fortune.

It's a litany of the forgetting that's a kind of remembering. He says:

> I forget the days in the auto plant
> doing seventy bodies per minute—
> the tools continuous in one loud scream,
> the pinch, punch, press, and pounding of steel—
> a gray space inside myself driven
> like a car to the next stop down the line.

I forget all the textbook recipes
and all the facts I never lived in school.
I forget the facts I lived: the wet kiss
in the heart of all events drying out.
I forget Worcester, Mass.; Oakland;
Lansing, Michigan; and Birmingham;
their industrial dream frozen in mid-air . . .

What I continue to ask myself: Was Gilbert forgotten because he wanted to be forgotten, or because we forgot him? He ends the stanza:

My face is a mask. Everyone wears it.
When I take it off there's another face.
I turn around to you, you this moment
I have come to empty-handed and not myself.

The image of the mask reappears in "The 'The'": "I try to place / myself among the facelessness, forms / whose abused use reduces / even my own bodily truths / to a mask." Gilbert often seems to be asking, *How can I be certain of my community, my world, when I'm not certain of myself?* It's the kind of unresolvable question explored in not so much a single poem as a body of work. It's the sort of quest that makes him some sort of Black Confessional Modernist. (I suppose we could just as well call it postmodernism, though for me the word always feels like a premature term for modernism.) Confessionalism in Gilbert is synonymous with transparency, with an "I" that is unashamed of its debt to experience and the difficulties of processing experience, especially black experience.

His style of modernism has some of Eliot's pomp and some of Stevens's aloofness; it has some of William Carlos Williams's ear for vernacular; it has some of Jean Toomer's pastoralism and Robert Hayden's textual densities. Everything is filtered through a subjective uncertainty that makes his concerns prescient and present and ours.

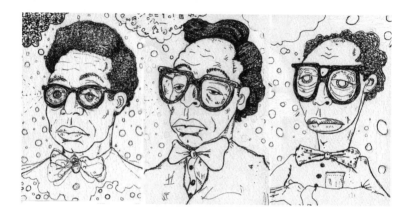

In "The Breathing / in / an Emancipatory Space," Gilbert's 1988 essay on Etheridge Knight, he provides the only explicit commentary I could find regarding his sense of poetry: "For the poet, . . . the startling feeling is how much we—as minds—are in the world rather than apart from it. . . . We are our situations." The remark seems in conversation with Lev Vygotsky's assertion that the mind is shaped through language and Ernst Cassirer's paradoxical notion that we flee ourselves even when we are seeking ourselves. It's not that we make words; it's that we are made of words. And because words are so unfixed, so amorphous, when we try to unmask ourselves through language, there is always another mask beneath the mask.

But this is not a problem for Gilbert. It's, as he says, a situation. If the face is a mask, we can remove it and wear any mask. The masks we wear make us mercurial, empathetic, imaginative. For example, in the poem echoing his debut's title, "Kodac and Chris Walking the Mutual Landscape," the speaker, so like Chris Gilbert his name is actually Chris, is out walking his dog and says to the dog: "Let's be simultaneous . . . because for once we both are beings . . . knowing nothing lives as a foreignness." Later in the poem he says, seeming to merge with the consciousness of the dog: "Let's begin being mutual . . . I'll be damned / if I don't step down in my neighbors' yards / with my mutt's paw and my situation / whole in the world." In Gilbert's poems, the self wanders a world that is not narrative, historical, or personal, but all of these things simultaneously: a situation.

A title such as "Listening to Monk's *Mysterioso* I Remember Braiding My Sisters' Hair" suggests the ways the poems in his debut *braid* situations. "Time with Stevie Wonder in It" demonstrates how his poems link a single moment to all its surrounding moments. Actually, the end of his first poem in *Across the Mutual Landscape*, "This Bridge Across," forecasts this aim: "each moment is a boundary / I will throw this bridge across." The space between the poet and the poem constitutes a moment; the space between the poem and the audience constitutes another.

■

Had there been no second book, we'd still have cause to meditate on the poetry of Chris Gilbert. Are you convinced yet? I mentioned a poem in which a dude morphs into his dog, y'all. In his elegy "Muriel Rukeyser as Energy," he imagines Muriel Rukeyser *as energy*, saying, "She is the speed of darkness— / witness her mystery, not her gown." Near the end of his masterful "Horizontal Cosmology," he turns himself into a bucket of rainwater set beside a trail you're passing: "I wish you luck," he writes, "you this world's blue thirst. You might be Malcolm X with one of Roethke's roses in your vest. You know the arithmetic of a double thirst. It's the same old loneliness that made Coltrane disappear. This time I'll be of use."

Had there been no second book, I would still be here saying it is not Poetry, maybe not even the poet, but the poem that matters most. The poem is the source of the most intimate interaction between poet and reader. The poem resists summary and blurbs, it asks for little more than air and ear to do its work.

When I opened the file Ed sent and read the title, *Chris Gilbert: An Improvisation (Music of the Striving That Was There)*, I said *Goddamn*. I mean: *Chris Gilbert: An Improvisation*. That title tells us everything. It embraces the confessional even while complicating it. It presents some-one improvising what it means to be Christopher Gilbert, a philosoph-ical wanderer full of a wry, blue wonder. In "Tourist," a poem from the first section ("Steps and Transformations"), he writes: "I am / into small steps here—I total the bits of me. / I have lived in countless places, childless, / without song."

The self is a tourist both displaced and situated in his displacement. Selfhood becomes an act of existential migration. Selfhood becomes as open as the gaps between language, between being and thinking, be-tween timelessness and time. The poet self strives to "build this lan-guage house. . . . This loving which lives outside time." The "language house" is one way of understanding the public library in the poem "The 'The.'" The language house is also one way of thinking about poetry and poetic community; the language house is shelter for the self that's searching and adrift.

One of the people I e-mailed after reading the new book was Jeff

Shotts, the Graywolf editor. Once he'd seen the poems and shared them with Mark Doty, they agreed to publish the new work with a reissue of *Across the Mutual Landscape* in Graywolf's Re/View Series. ("The Re/View Series brings all-but-lost masterworks of recent American poetry into the hands of a new generation of readers.") As we mulled over a title that could bridge both collections, the end of "Turning into Dwelling" came back to me:

> Lord, the anguish of my Black block rises up in me
> like a grief. My only chance to go beyond being breach—
> to resist being quelled as a bit of inner-city entropy—
> is to speak up for the public which has birthed me.
> To build this language house. To make this case. Create.
> This loving which lives outside time. Lord, this is time.

"Turning into Dwelling" embodies Gilbert's obsession with the space, the breach between restlessness and stability, inside and outside, closed and open, public and private. His poetry makes "turning" both a gesture and an act of transformation; it makes "dwelling" both a shelter and an act of rumination. "The 'The'" begins:

> At closing time,
> standing outside the public library
> with ID card expired,
> the books remain on shelves—
> Lev Vygotsky, Toni Morrison, Levertov, Cassirer,
> and the Zora Neale Hurston (which probably isn't there) . . .

In seeing what this unidentified seeker seeks we see something of the seeker. It's a wonderfully diverse list, but the authors share a concern for culture and community. Finding the public library—the community language shelter—closed, the seeker says:

> I feel like some third person
> locked outside the language
> through which I am
> the things I mean.

Outside the library, Christopher Gilbert creates a language that insists on his place as well as his displacement. I say this is a version of Christopher Gilbert, because Christopher Gilbert says it is Christopher Gilbert. "i am absolutely / the I in the writing" he says in "Into the Into," but he writes it with an atypical lowercase *i* as if to suggest he nonetheless struggles to dwell inside and outside his writing, his communities, his self/selves. The poems strike me as urgent because of his isolation; the poet strikes me as tragic because of his isolation. I won't say "lonely." I don't know whether he was lonely. Though there were no other books, Christopher Gilbert maintained his links to poetry and poets, at least through the 1980s. In 1986, after receiving a National Endowment for the Arts fellowship in poetry, he took the year off and was poet-in-residence at the Robert Frost Center in New Hampshire, as well as a visiting poet at the University of Pittsburgh. *Contemporary Authors* Online Biography Resource Center cites Gilbert explaining how the time off was necessary for his poems: "I feel that my own ability to write poetry wants this; it wants its experience to be grounded in the firsthand world gained through contact with lives and people, with me —as subject—as an empathy, with a reflection toward one's deeper and longer life, with goals, with a concept of use." One hears his desire to be less isolated, to find community and purpose.

The penultimate section of "Into the Into," one of the last poems in *Chris Gilbert: An Improvisation*, works quite explicitly to explore or reconcile the ambitions he set for himself.

i am a passing thing
in which i am a subject—
read my lines, be my mind.
i am absolutely
the I in the writing,
the dead refuse to sing.

Where he'd set a goal to be "subject—as an empathy" for community, he inevitably calls out for the empathy *of* community: "read my lines, be my mind." "Into the Into" is almost a somber presage of the next decade's blocks or silences or refusals. When I emailed Elizabeth Alexander about Gilbert, she said she'd never met him, but she knew his work. She'd called him a few years before he died, wanting to include him in an anthology: "He was quiet, said he'd been dealing with chronic illness. Not friendly but not unfriendly. Said he had new poems but never sent them." She ended the message with a very earnest question: "Maybe he is the most original poet of his generation? Possible."

By the early 1990s, Gilbert was a psychology professor at Bristol Community College in Fall River, Massachusetts. Whatever the difficulties—illness, doubt, discouragement—Gilbert's poems remained in the world. In the remarkable title poem, "Chris Gilbert: An Improvisation," someone so like Christopher Gilbert he calls himself Christopher Gilbert is in the hospital after one of the surgeries that, as we now know, will ultimately not save him.

CHRIS GILBERT: AN IMPROVISATION

The writing on the half-filled helium balloon says,
"Get Well Soon." A few days from getting out of the hospital,
I'm trying to make the balloon float again

while I watch the body of Lt. Col. William Higgins somewhere
in Lebanon swing from its noose on the TV news.
High on Cyclosporine, Prednisone, Imuran, Nefedipine,
Zantac, Tenormin, Lasix, and Persantine, I toss
the balloon on its tether toward the tepid air
around the TV where Dan Rather's voice rises,
though it is as cloaked in lifelessness as the corpse
it describes, which, even as it swings, is getting
hardened into a media thing, a factual because
it's no longer filled with the ponderous void that living brings.
A weight fills me as I allow myself to think
that being alive is hard work, full of just this
human future which, in the light of Higgins, hits me
as an emptiness I make promises of to lift my spirit with.
As I watch TV I imagine the kidney I've been given is
Higgins's, but now my nurse comes in with more medicine
and juice to swallow this with, and stories of how her shift
has been, and promises of a backrub later that, though
it might not show what will become of me as it really is,
does distinguish my next few hours or so from his.
So for this moment I take this strange white setting
and its alien equipment, my nurse, and even my new body
and its present distinctions as parts of a momentary thing
pursuing its momentary meaning, or else—like Higgins—
hardening into a loss or ending. I am reaching to get through
the frozen doors of these stagnant facts, to sully the present
happy affliction with lack, with becoming, or some
unfinished act to show the consequences of where I'm at.
So tonight when the team from hematology troops in
to take my blood again, asking if I'm the transplant patient,

and I go mum because I've gone through this twice
daily now for two weeks, my family who will be
visiting and who will have helped me into whatever
state of mind I am will clear the air for me to declare
I am. The IV unit with my name and directions for my care
taped to the top will indicate I am. The ID bracelet
I've been wearing since I got here will say for me,
"I am." The scar the surgeon left as a signature
on my belly's right side will say, "I am." I am
I feel a gathering possibility passing from temporary
articulation to articulation the way the horizon
arises in the sun as a series of evident illuminations
while the earth spins clockwise toward futurity.
When the time comes I'll rise and say, "I am."
I'll gather all my questions, step into their midst
and say, "I am." I am I am.

I assumed the poem was truly the last of his poems, a breathtaking self-
elegy written near his death in 2007, after a twenty-year battle against
polycystic kidney disease. I thought, yes, Christopher Gilbert was beau-
tifully striving "to be" even when there was no poetic community to in-
habit. I was ready for some aspiring mythmaking. Then, out of curiosity I googled "Lt. Col. William Higgins" and read he was captured by
Hezbollah while serving on a United Nations peacekeeping mission in
Lebanon in 1988. He'd been hanged by his captors in 1990. The detail
deeply depressed me. It left me with little to fill that seventeen-year gap
following Gilbert's decade of productivity and aspirations to build community. Some days I assure myself he continued working, but it's hard
to know. I like to imagine him fine-tuning, dismantling and reassem-

bling the book as if it was a self meant to endure. There were nine or ten versions left to Fran Quinn and Mary Fell, who, according to Fran, ordered them into a final set. (I still don't know the role Gilbert's wife played in any of this.)

It's not that I think an organization like Cave Canem or a really great poet friend would have helped Gilbert write through the 1990s. It's not that *completely*, at least. It's a question of our obligations not just to the people within our circle but also to those outside. We don't have to look very far to find poets prizing and protecting and endlessly complicating what it means to belong to a community of black poets. Cave Canem fellows and teachers, one must assume, ascribe to the organization's mission as "a home for the many voices of African American poetry." But bringing "many voices" together means that notions of poetry, blackness, and even solidarity are constantly being challenged and expanded. How does the multiplicity of voices change the "fundamental blackness" that unifies Cave Canem as a community? What is our obligation to those poets who remain for whatever reason outside even our most diverse communities? What are we going to do about/with/for that other psychologist poet working out there, his name might be Forrest Hamer; what are we going to do about/with/for Thylias Moss, Will Alexander; what should we have done about/with/for Wanda Coleman, Ai, Russell Atkins? Gilbert's struggle was, perhaps, any poet's struggle, to maintain both a willful essential individuality and a sense of community. I'm not quite able to say what that community looked like for him or any of the poet's I've named.

Michael Harper, who selected *Across the Mutual Landscape* for the 1983 Walt Whitman Award, was one of the first poets I e-mailed in 2010 to ask about Gilbert. Harper has never failed to acknowledge his muses and mentors—Sterling A. Brown and Robert Hayden, most especially —but he has also been muse and mentor for many. He told me Gilbert had died of an "inherited kidney problem" and that, as an undergraduate, he'd studied with Robert Hayden at the University of Michigan.

I can't help but wonder how much Gilbert was shaped by his relationships with Hayden, the austere formalist, with Harper, the jazz progressive, and with Knight, the restless bluesman. Gilbert, born in Birmingham, Alabama, was, like Knight, a southern transplant; Gilbert, like Hayden, was raised in industrial Detroit; Gilbert, like Harper, lived much of his adult life in Providence, Rhode Island. I can't help but wonder how many great stories he could have shared about them. He dwelled at the borders of many poetic, cultural, and intellectual communities. It's possible he was absorbed by the spaces between those borders: "the ponderous void that living brings." I think of him and his poems somehow always here and not here at the edge of our community. That is to say, his poems have never seemed abandoned or forgotten or disregarded. They seem to have anticipated his family, friends, and fans striving as he strove:

> To build this language house. To make this case. Create.
> This loving which lives outside time. Lord, this is time.

LINE 38: I AM ME

Later I dreamed I was on a night plane somewhere between the stars and Indianapolis. It was a crow's sky: ominous, black, sparkling. The man across the aisle, he sounded African, talked to a drowsy white woman about something that frequently featured the words *Obama* and *Oh, Mamma*. It was none of my business. When I looked down from the plane window, I saw cemetery shapes. The African said to the drowsy woman, "It is not often an African marries an American white woman, but when it happens our offspring rules the free world." I heard him say "cost of living," and "Yeah," and "Thank you, Lord" when our plane touched ground.

I visited Indianapolis once in my waking life. Nearly fifteen years after Etheridge Knight's death, I'd arrived with a satchel of books and questions, invited by Knight's sister, Eunice, to read my poems at the Etheridge Knight Festival. When I spoke with her about her brother for a few hours in a downtown hotel, she let me record our conversation. She wore a blue headscarf and shared her cigarettes with me. I'd already decided a biography needed to be written and that I would not be the one to write it. My aim was to gather stories his future biographer could use.

I know I should not admit I was dreaming. Vision being what it is in a dream, from a distance I thought the driver awaiting me near baggage claim was none other than three-time NCAA championship coach

Bobby Knight. Nearer I saw he was actually James Whitcomb Riley, the nineteenth-century poet. Age of Henry Wadsworth Longfellow, William Cullen Bryant, James Russell Lowell: something sumptuous in a three-word name. Old James Whitcomb Riley struggled a bit dragging my book-heavy bags to the trunk of a sedan longer and blacker than a hearse.

That first trip to Indy, Eunice told me Junior, the family's nickname for Knight, loved no one more than he loved his mother. After an hour or so Eunice took me to the Crown Hill Cemetery. As the third- or fourth-largest cemetery in the country, it's a storehouse, a ghost archive to more than 190,000 names. "This will help me get my bearing," Eunice said from the hilltop where the grand, white columns of James Whitcomb Riley's tomb loomed at the highest point in the city. She scanned the acres of headstones around us, adjusting her eyeglasses as if they were binoculars as she looked for her brother. She was happy, I think, that I had come, maybe the first ever to come asking her brother's story. My bags waited downhill in a pickup truck with an obese, melancholy white woman, Eunice's daughter-in-law. The plump biracial girl in the backseat was Eunice's grandchild. Eunice called out plot numbers, swinging her cigarette in various directions like a smoldering conductor's wand, as if she were casting some sort of spell. And I could see she was proud to show me the Riley tomb. It's possible any out-of-towner visiting Crown Hill for the first time is shown the Hoosier Poet's resting place. It's possible countless Indiana children have taken field trips to visit the Hoosier Poet every year since his death in 1916.

That day at least partly explained my driver in the dream. *Hoosier* made me think of basketball, Bobby Knight in bright-red face and sweater berating a referee or a pale player with a crew cut. I imagined

James Whitcomb Riley as someone resembling Bobby Knight when Eunice recited the beginning of Riley's most well-known poem to assure me I'd heard of him. I didn't recognize the poem. I've forgotten its lines. It occurred to me: perhaps Bobby Knight had been pretending to be the Hoosier Poet after all.

In the dream, I'd already decided a biography of Etheridge Knight needed to be written and flew to Indianapolis, one of his haunts, to begin it. I'd need to fact-check everything about a man with a slippery relationship to facts. In the bags with me in the dream were files, outlines, interviews, books, journals, essays, and essay fragments. My life was always interrupted when I turned to Knight's life. Plus whenever I thought about the specter of writing a biography, I was overcome with fear. Knight was a good talker. I am a good talker, but I have no sense of plot, really. And I generally prefer imagination over research. I had not visited Kentucky, where a biographical plot features the young Knight as a runaway, a black Huck Finn, and could be researched; I had not visited Korea, where a biographical plot features the young Knight as a seventeen-year-old soldier and runaway, and could be researched; I had not visited the Indiana State Penitentiary where a biographical plot features the young Knight as an inmate and could be researched; and most significantly, I had not visited Corinth, Mississippi, where Knight was born.

The various plots of Corinth include its namesake, the Greek city-state destroyed by Rome in 146 BC. The plots of Corinth include the year 1854, when a railroad town development called Cross City was renamed Corinth. The plots of Corinth include the ghosts of the 473 Rebel soldiers killed in the Second Battle of Corinth during the American Civil War. Sometimes you can have no more than an idea of history's plots. Plots are filled with dirt and antiquated clothes, with black landowners just out of earshot of the train whistles and dereliction. The various plots of Corinth include Knight's mother, Belzora, breathing the wide, free, green air at the turn of the century. "My mother always wore shoes," Eunice told me. "They raised everything they needed." Even the whites called her grandfather "Mister Cozart." This, Eunice said, this was the privilege her brother was born into in 1931. The privilege he wanted all his life, she says.

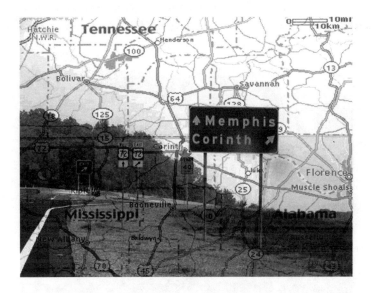

On the back of Knight's *Born of a Woman: New and Selected Poems*, is a photo Ellen Slack took of Knight with his kinsfolk during a 1979 visit to Mississippi. (These drawings are based on that photo.) Gray-haired Mr. Pink Knight and Etheridge wear overalls. Mr. Pink Knight stoops behind three young girls peering at the camera. Etheridge Knight seems to be looking off, across a field perhaps, caught in midsentence. The light reflected in the wide lenses of his eyeglasses makes his eyes two white bursts below his newsboy cap. The three girls pose exactly as they would have for an elementary school photo. Mr. Pink Knight seems to be rising from the porch behind him. A woman stands just over his shoulder peering down from the porch with a hand resting on her rotund waist—a pose that is both maternal and amused. A few feet behind her a second, much thinner, woman stands with her arms crossed; her face is washed out by the shadows. She seems headless, apparitional, a slightly perturbed ghost in a white dress. They are perhaps the two aunts Knight mentions in "The Idea of Ancestry."

Slack's photo also appears in the 1988 issue of *Painted Bride Quarterly* dedicated to Knight. Slack says, "Etheridge had heard that his relative Pink Knight was staying with family in that vicinity, and he wanted me to take some photographs. . . . No birth records existed for Pink Knight, but by all accounts he had to be at least 110 years old, meaning he was born in Mississippi shortly after the end of the Civil War." Knight wanted to record the plots and plights of his oldest living ancestor. He wanted more than an idea of ancestry. A Corinth, Mississippi, plot includes Etheridge Knight smiling in the photo. I once thought a life was simply the accumulation of details. Maybe I think this even now. Knight was often blowing smoke over details. And to write a biography, one would need to gather all that smoke into something solid, something you could hold and turn over in your hands.

Time, patience, and discipline are irrelevant in a dream. I should not admit it was a dream: I reached the same hotel I'd stayed in to interview

Eunice years before; I arrived after midnight with a satchel of books, seeking stories of the poet's life on earth. I did not sleep. There was an old but functional typewriter in my room. The housekeeper said each room had paper and a typewriter. "We like to call them pianos," she told me. The first time I'd stayed there—when I was awake and real—Eunice said the hotel had been a haunt for black writers like Mari Evans.

Mari Evans, born the summer of 1923, author of several poetry books, children books, and plays, was still alive somewhere in Indianapolis until March 2017. As further evidence of my lousy research and biographer skills, I didn't meet her. But in the dream, she worked the desk and wore an ornate water-colored dress, reciting her best-known

poem, "I Am a Black Woman," to anyone who looked like the wrong sort of guest: anyone who was used to talking more than listening, anyone who did not look you in the eye when looking you in the face. She did not hand me my room key until the poem's dramatic ending: "beyond all definition still / defying place / and time / and circumstance / assailed / impervious / indestructible / Look / on me and be / renewed."

I did not sleep. Each time I closed my door or eyes someone showed up to offer a tale about Knight. A woman who looked no more than twenty-five years old wanted to tell me about the day she spent with Etheridge in 1956. One of my own teachers, Ed Ochester, appeared with a tale of big Beefeater bottles and a whole pig roasting on a spit at the wake Knight held for himself. Poets Robert Bly, Sharon Olds, and Christopher Gilbert showed up to share poems. Jeanne D'Amico stopped by to tell me a version of the story she'd told me when I interviewed her in my waking life. Knight's leg was amputated after a car wreck in Philadelphia in 1988. In the dream she told me the tracks and scars glowed like half-lit embers in the darkness of his body. His face was swollen and more than half dead, but he still had that voice like burlap soaked in molasses. She handed me a small, silver ring and made me promise to place it on the shy, black pinky toe of Knight's remaining foot when I met him.

An old man named Hound Mouth promised I'd be brought to Knight after undertaking a special task. Hound Mouth had spent years gathering the piles of butts left by Etheridge. He organized them into categories: cigarettes smoked in prison, cigarettes smoked after making love, cigarettes smoked in Tennessee, in Massachusetts, in Minnesota, cigarettes smashed under boots, cigarettes tossed into rivers. He had no research to prove they should have been ordered in this way.

He'd just held each butt to his nose or to the light and then let his intuition decide its place. My task was to match specific butts to specific poems. I sat with him for what felt like half an eternity just looking at it all. I had a little tape recorder with me. I ate a little corner of Hound Mouth's ham-and-cheese sandwich. I sat twice as long the next day.

Eventually Hound Mouth gave up on me. In the dream he confessed Knight was still alive and incarcerated in an assisted-living facility across town. We came to a security guard at a small desk in the building's cavernous lounge. When Hound Mouth told me the guard was Knight's only son, Isaac BuShie Blackburn-Knight, I blurted almost without thinking, "I liked *sons* better than *children*." "Yeah, me too," he said, looking down. During my waking visit to Indianapolis, Eunice told me someone casually suggested *children* for the end of "The Idea of Ancestry," so Knight had changed it from *sons* to *children*. *Sons* is not the same as *children*. Sons are not soft amorphous offspring. Sons are born with knives or pistols; pissing and pointing because they are sons. God only had sons, according to Christians. That tells you some of the trouble with God. Sons are both old and brand-new. Sons are miniature men. But *children* are as generic as *people*: sometimes horribly innocent, sometimes horribly attractive, and sometimes horrible. Children have no gender. It is false but widely believed that children are universal. It is only true that children are universal if *universal* means "full of space." Space is expansive, impermanent, and mysterious. Knight lived with children who were not his children. They had names and nicknames before he met them. But there is little on record about the children because they are thought of as children. The children become invisible. Because the adults are looking elsewhere, but also because the children do not wish to be seen. They were sons before they were children, in the poem "The Idea of Ancestry." Farmers, soldiers, preachers wearing Knight's name with a princely carriage. He dreamed of them inside the cell. He sat in the dark with a premonition of the damage that would befall his sons. He would have to abandon them to make them stronger. He would have to change them to children.

The suggestion to change the line from "I have no sons" to "I have no children" came before Knight had a son, but now here was his son: half black, half white, a lobby guard with a goatee thick and wooly as a surgical mask. I could not see his face. In my waking life, I'd wondered often about the boy's appearance and whereabouts. Did he have his mother's mouth and nose? Did he have siblings? Did he imagine his father's ghost was with him when he graduated from high school or college or was admitted to an emergency room with a broken bone? Did he know he was the son of a poet? Had he grown up reading his father's books? Had he shunned the books stacked tall and smelling of difficulty and tobacco? Had the son seen the photograph of his father in the Half-Lotus Tree yoga pose in a Las Vegas tuxedo shop before the 1987 American Book Award? Did the son possess photographs of his father's dark, sleeping head and unzipped, oblivious mouth? Did the son rage or weep in his sleep? He'd be a man now with children of his own, but I had done none of the research needed to find him.

In the dream, the watchman was Isaac BuShie Blackburn-Knight. He nodded and let me pass. The building had more floors than there were stars over the city. The elevator ride up was so long I dozed off and dreamed I was being driven north by my little brother. He was telling me a tale about a soldier who had given a testimonial in church one Sunday. He'd been a prisoner of war, bound in the cellar of a farmer and his wife. "I was saved by a black dog, a hound whose master had probably been killed in the war," the soldier told the dumbstruck congregation, my brother among them. "For a moment I thought the dog was no more than a lean shadow in the corner: a darkness slipping over the antiques and contraptions of my captors. But then the dog pulled the rope from my wrists and ankles. When he touched his cool muzzle to my jaw, I knew he wished to lead me away. I crawled through the cellar window behind him, and then too tired to rise, followed on my hands and knees through the fields and into a deep, dark forest. Had anyone seen me, they would have thought a dog was following a dog."

We were between borders on a mountain highway when my brother told the story. Before this trip, I had not been alone with him for that

long since childhood. There was a black train in the distance. I pray for you, my brother said to me. After a year of marriage he had changed, as a man bound by love or grief is bound to change. Their first child had not survived. He had laid his sorrows down and put on a new name. Sundays now, the preacher came to dine. I wanted to ask a few questions. White fog covered the nose of the car. I was falling into the kind of sleep that requires no darkness. "He reached our church with a look that reminded me of you," my brother said to me. "We thought he'd come that day to give thanks to God, but he'd come to ask who among us was his kin."

SELECTED BIBLIOGRAPHY

Alexander, Elizabeth. *The Black Interior: Essays*. Saint Paul, MN: Graywolf, 2004.

Ames, Fisher. *Works of Fisher Ames with a Selection from His Speeches and Correspondence*. Ed. Seth Ames. Boston: Little, Brown and Company, 1854.

Anaporte-Easton, Jean, editor. *Callaloo* 19 (Fall 1996: Special section on Etheridge Knight).

Baca, Jimmy Santiago. *Immigrants in Our Own Land: Poems*. Baton Rouge: Louisiana State University Press, 1979.

Baraka, Amiri (with Larry Neal). *Black Fire: An Anthology of Afro-American Writing*. New York: Morrow, 1968.

———. *SOS: Poems 1961–2013*, edited by Paul Vangelisti. New York: Grove Press, 2015.

Barthes, Roland. *A Lover's Discourse: Fragments*. London: Penguin, 1978.

Bauman, Zygmunt. *Liquid Modernity*. Cambridge, UK: Polity, 2000.

Baxandall, Michael. *Patterns of Intention: On the Historical Explanation of Pictures*. New Haven: Yale University Press, 1985.

Bly, Robert. *The Man in the Black Coat Turns: Poems*. New York: Harper & Row Perennial Library, 1988.

Boyd, Melba Joyce. *Wrestling with the Muse: Dudley Randall and the Broadside Press*. New York: Columbia University Press, 2003.

Brooks, Gwendolyn. *In the Mecca: Poems*. New York: Harper & Row, 1968.

Camp, Louis (with Joanna DiPaolo and Louis McKee), editors. *Painted Bride Quarterly* (Number 32/33: Etheridge Knight Issue), 1988.

Chekhov, Anton. "Gooseberries," from *Short Stories*. Translated by Constance Garnett. New York: Macmillan, 1928.

Clifton, Lucille. *Good Times: Poems*. New York: Random House, 1969.

Coleman, Wanda. *Mercurochrome: New Poems*. Santa Rosa, CA: Black Sparrow, 2001.

Collins, Michael S., and Linda Wagner-Martin. *Understanding Etheridge Knight*. Columbia, SC: University of South Carolina Press, 2012.

Derricotte, Toi. *Captivity*. Pittsburgh, PA: University of Pittsburgh, 1989.

Epstein, Andrew. *Beautiful Enemies: Friendship and Postwar American Poetry*. Oxford (England)/New York: Oxford University Press, 2006.

Freytag, Gustav. *Technique of the Drama: An Exposition of Dramatic Composition and Art*. Translated by Elias J. MacEwan. New York: B. Blom, 1968.

Gass, William H. *On Being Blue: A Philosophical Inquiry*. New York: The New York Review of Books, 2014.

Gilbert, Christopher. *Across the Mutual Landscape*. Port Townsend, WA: Graywolf, 1984.

———. *Turning into Dwelling*. Graywolf Poetry Re/View Series. Graywolf, 2015.

Hoagland, Tony. *What Narcissism Means to Me*. Saint Paul, MN: Graywolf, 2003.

Hughes, Langston. *The Early Simple Stories*. Edited by Donna Sullivan Harper. Columbia, MO: University of Missouri Press, 2002.

———. "The Negro Artist and the Racial Mountain," *The Nation* 122 (June 23, 1926): 692–694.

———. *The Panther and the Lash: Poems of Our Times*. New York: Knopf, 1967.

Johnson, Steven. *Where Good Ideas Come From: The Natural History of Innovation*. New York: Riverhead, 2010.

Knight, Etheridge. *Belly Song and Other Poems*. Detroit: Broadside, 1973.

———. *Black Voices from Prison*. New York: Pathfinder, 1970.

———. *Born of a Woman: New and Selected Poems*. Boston: Houghton Mifflin, 1980.

———. *The Essential Etheridge Knight.* Pittsburgh, PA: University of Pittsburgh Press, 1986.

———. "My Father, My Bottom, My Fleas," *Negro Digest* (August 1966).

———. "On the Next Train South," *Negro Digest* (June 1967).

———. *Poems from Prison.* Detroit: Broadside, 1968.

———. "Reaching Is His Rule," *Negro Digest* (December 1965).

Lorde, Audre. *The Collected Poems of Audre Lorde.* New York: W. W. Norton, 2002.

Lowell, Robert. *Life Studies.* New York: Farrar, Straus and Cudahy, 1959.

Nabokov, Vladimir. *Pale Fire.* New York: Perigee, 1980.

Neal, Larry, Amiri Baraka, and Michael Schwartz. *Visions of a Liberated Future: Black Arts Movement Writings.* New York: Thunder's Mouth, 1989.

O'Connor, Flannery. *A Good Man Is Hard to Find and Other Stories.* Orlando, FL: Harcourt, 1983.

Ozick, Cynthia. *Quarrel & Quandary: Essays.* New York: Knopf, 2000.

Rampersad, Arnold. *The Life of Langston Hughes, Vol. I, 1902–1941: I, Too, Sing America.* New York: Oxford University Press, 1986.

———. *The Life of Langston Hughes, Vol. II, 1941–1967, I Dream a World.* New York: Oxford University Press, 1988.

Rankine, Claudia. *Citizen: An American Lyric.* Minneapolis, MN: Graywolf, 2014.

Robinson, Marilynne. *When I Was a Child I Read Books.* New York: Farrar, Straus and Giroux, 2012.

Schuyler, George S. "The Negro-Art Hokum," *The Nation* 122 (June 16, 1926): 662–3.

Shaywitz, David A., and Douglas A. Melton. "The Molecular Biography of the Cell." *Cell,* Vol. 120, Issue 6, 729–731.

Stewart, Susan. *On Longing: Narratives of the Miniature, the Gigantic, the Souvenir, the Collection.* Baltimore, MD: Johns Hopkins University Press, 1984.

Szymborska, Wisława. "Children of our Age," from *Poems New and Collected, 1957–1997*. Translated by Stanisław Barańczak and Clare Cavanagh. New York: Harcourt Brace, 1998.

Taylor, Henry. *The Flying Change: Poems*. Baton Rouge: Louisiana State University Press, 1985.

Wordsworth, William. *Essential Wordsworth*. Selected and with an introduction by Seamus Heaney. New York: Ecco Press, 1988.

ACKNOWLEDGMENTS

The Bagley Wright Lecture Series on Poetry supports contemporary poets as they explore in-depth their own thinking on poetry and poetics, and give a series of lectures resulting from these investigations.

This work evolved from lectures given at the following institutions:

"Turning into Dwelling: The Space Between the Poet and the Poem," Cave Canem, Brooklyn, NY, October 9, 2014; "Ideas of Influence," Library of Congress, Washington, DC, January 22, 2015; "Three Acts of Love," New York University, New York, NY, March 13, 2015; "Poems from Prison," The Poetry Foundation, Chicago, IL, April 2, 2015; "Poetics of Liquid," Seattle Arts & Lectures, Seattle, WA, May 5, 2015; "DIY For Langston Hughes," Bread Loaf, Middlebury, VT, August 12, 2015.

Thank you to Nicole Sealey at Cave Canem, Rob Casper at the Library of Congress, April Heck at NYU, Stephen Young at the Poetry Foundation, Rebecca Hoogs at Seattle Arts and Lectures, and Bread Loaf (under the directorship of Michael Collier and Jennifer Grotz), and their respective staffs, for welcoming the Bagley Wright Lecture Series into their programming, and for collaborating on scheduling, promoting, introducing, and recording these events. The Series would be impossible without such partners.

NOTE FROM THE AUTHOR

Gratitude to the editors who published earlier versions of these works: *Callaloo*; *The Enchanting Verses Literary Review*; *Guernica*; *Poet Lore*; *Poetry Magazine*; *Soul Soldiers: African Americans and the Vietnam Era*; *Turning into Dwelling*.

"Knight's Vest of Selves" was inspired by Jon Sands' poem "Decoded." The drawing on page 198 is based on a photograph by Elizabeth McKim that appears on page 3 of the Etheridge Knight issue of the *Painted Bride Quarterly*.

A big bow of thanks to the Wave Books crew, Heidi Broadhead, Joshua Beckman, and especially, Matthew Zapruder, for your patience, guidance, and constant encouragement; to the University of Pittsburgh, the NYU Distinguished Residency, the Passa Porta Residency for time; to Pitt Press for keeping *The Essential Etheridge Knight* in print; to Charles Rowell and Michael Collier for thinking deeply about Etheridge; to Jean Anaporte-Easton for keeping your camera on Etheridge; to Elizabeth McKim for sharing your time and love for Etheridge; to Ed Ochester for remaining a friend, teacher, and fount of Etheridge stories; to Mary Karr, who was among the first I interviewed about Etheridge, for heart and incomparable company; to Eunice Knight-Bowens, who passed in 2013, for more than can be said about Etheridge, eternally; to Radiclani Clytus, Joel Dias-Porter, and Yusef Komunyakaa for your beautiful shades of Etheridgeness; to Elizabeth Alexander for remaining by my heart and ear; and to Yona Harvey for family, for everything, always.

A lifetime of acknowledgments to those who keep Etheridge's name alive.